•THE 9th LIST
•OF SHIT
•THAT MADE
•ME A
•FEMINIST

Farida D.

Farida D. is an Arab gender researcher and poet, studying Arab women's everyday oppressions for over a decade. Through the process- she broke up with her hijab, set her high heels on fire, and authored a series of books. Farida's words have been on BBC Radio London, are continuously amplified by celebrities, and strolling all over social media. Contact her via email farida-d@outlook.com, or on Instagram @farida.d.author

This is for the women
living in a "man's world".
The women who scream
for us to be heard.

1601.

Capitalism creates poverty
in the same way that
patriarchy creates misogyny
in the same way that
White supremacy creates racism
in the same way that
heteronormativity creates homophobia.

Because when we uphold
one socially constructed system
as absolute truth without void-
all exceptions
are destroyed.

***

Misogyny doesn't exist because of women;
it exists because of patriarchy.
Homophobia doesn't exist because of homosexual people;
it exists because of heteronormativity.
Racism doesn't exist because of non-White people;
it exists because of White supremacy.

The oppressed cannot be held accountable for oppression.

1602.

We live in a world
where being a misogynist
is more acceptable
than being a feminist,
where being homophobic
is more acceptable
than being homosexual,
where being a racist
is more acceptable
than being Black.
We live in a world
where being privileged
means your *opinion*
is acceptable
as a *fact*.

1603.

History repeats itself
only when told by the oppressor
who holds the power
to repeatedly oppress.

***

There is no
right or wrong;
only
oppressor or oppressed.

1604.

Not every man is a misogynist,
but every man benefits from misogyny.

Not every cisgender person is transphobic,
but every cisgender person benefits from transphobia.

Not every heterosexual person is homophobic,
but every heterosexual person benefits from homophobia.

Not every White person is a racist,
but every White person benefits from racism.

Not every abled person is an ableist,
but every abled person benefits from ableism.

It isn't your fault what your ancestors built
but you *still* benefit
from being favoured
by having the world catered
to you at the expense of others.

And when you refuse to acknowledge this
you continue to contribute
to how the oppressed suffer.

***

Every cishet man
is born out of
an oppressed body.

Every privilege
is born out of
oppressing somebody.

1605.

Maybe you're a man who has never discriminated against a woman, but surely you've benefited from being favoured over her. Maybe you've never hurt a woman, but surely you've benefited from laws that hurt her to protect you. Maybe you've never disrespected a woman, but surely you've benefited from being the "nice guy" for doing bare minimum. Maybe you're not a misogynist, but you surely benefit from misogyny. Maybe you think it's not your fault, but you surely benefit from the problem. And maybe you're wondering what the solution is, but I surely hope you start by realizing that it is ALL MEN- and you are one of them.

***

Maybe you're a non-Black person who has never discriminated against a Black person, but surely you've benefited from being favoured over them. Maybe you've never hurt a Black person, but surely you've benefited from laws that hurt them to protect you. Maybe you've never disrespected a Black person, but surely you've benefited from being the "nice person" for doing bare minimum. Maybe you're not a racist, but you surely benefit from racism. Maybe you think it's not your fault, but you surely benefit from the problem. And maybe you're wondering what the solution is, but I surely hope you start by realizing that it is ALL NON-BLACK PEOPLE- and you are one of them.

***

Maybe you're a heterosexual person who has never discriminated against a homosexual person, but surely you've benefited from being favoured over them. Maybe you've never hurt a homosexual person, but surely you've benefited from laws that hurt them to protect you. Maybe you've never disrespected a homosexual person, but surely you've benefited from being the "nice person" for doing bare minimum. Maybe you're not homophobic, but you surely benefit from homophobia. Maybe you think it's not your fault, but you surely benefit from the problem. And maybe you're wondering what the solution is, but I surely hope you start by realizing that it is ALL HETEROSEXUAL PEOPLE- and you are one of them.

***

Maybe you're a cisgender person who has never discriminated against a transgender person, but surely you've benefited from being favoured over them. Maybe you've never hurt a transgender person, but surely you've benefited from laws that hurt them to protect you. Maybe you've never disrespected a transgender person, but surely you've benefited from being the "nice person" for doing bare minimum. Maybe you're not transphobic, but you surely benefit from transphobia. Maybe you think it's not your fault, but you surely benefit from the problem. And maybe you're wondering what the solution is, but I surely hope you start by realizing that it is ALL CISGENDER PEOPLE- and you are one of them.

***

Maybe you're an abled person who has never discriminated against a disabled person, but surely you've benefited from being favoured over them. Maybe you've never hurt a disabled person, but surely you've benefited from laws that hurt them to protect you. Maybe you've never disrespected a disabled person, but surely you've benefited from being the "nice person" for doing bare minimum. Maybe you're not an ableist, but you surely benefit from ableism. Maybe you think it's not your fault, but you surely benefit from the problem. And maybe you're wondering what the solution is, but I surely hope you start by realizing that it is ALL ABLED PEOPLE- and you are one of them.

***

Maybe you're a rich person who has never discriminated against a poor person, but surely you've benefited from being favoured over them. Maybe you've never hurt a poor person, but surely you've benefited from laws that hurt them to protect you. Maybe you've never disrespected a poor person, but surely you've benefited from being the "nice person" for doing bare minimum. Maybe you're not a classist, but you surely benefit from classism. Maybe you think it's not your fault, but you surely benefit from the problem. And maybe you're wondering what the solution is, but I surely hope you start by realizing that it is ALL RICH PEOPLE- and you're one of them.

***

Are you tired of *reading* the same thing
again and again?

Good.

There are people that are tired of *living* the same thing
again and again.

1606.

Hamas exists
because of Zionists,
and Zionists exist
because of antisemitism,
and antisemitism exists
because of White supremacy,
and White supremacy exists
because of racism,
and racism exists
because of oppressors,
and those oppressors are also
heteronormative, patriarchal,
classist, and ableist,
and they will continue to exist-
so long as we don't
hold them accountable,
for how all of this fits.

N.B. Calling out Israel is not antisemitism. Calling out Hamas is not
Islamophobia.

1607.

I am Jewish when it's Hanukkah.
I am Christian when it's Christmas.
I am Muslim when it's Eid.

And wherever there is celebration
you will find me there.

N.B. Celebrate humanity.

1608.

No we aren't all the same.

We are of different race, gender, sex
and whatever else
that is essentially socially constructed nonsense
but has led to real consequence
nonetheless.

And it doesn't make you a racist or a sexist
if you acknowledge that we live in a world
that *created* those differences.

The racist and sexist
are the ones who assign *different value to those differences*
the ones who categorize our differences
as superior/inferior and good/bad;
we all deserve the same opportunities
despite what our ancestors got or never had.

When we stop categorizing our differences under a binary
and instead start viewing ourselves under one branch of humanity
our differences won't matter eventually-
we will return to who we used to be
before being branded
by White supremacy.

1609.

Capitalism invents low wage jobs
and then looks down upon people who work in them.

Patriarchy invents women's sexual objectification
and then looks down upon women who embrace their sexual being.

Heteronormativity invents homophobia
and then looks down upon people who are homosexual.

White supremacy invents racism
and then looks down upon anyone who isn't White.

Who invented your oppression?
How are they using shame to stop you from dismantling the system?

***

Misogyny was invented to uphold patriarchy.
Homophobia was invented to uphold heteronormativity.
Racism was invented to uphold White supremacy.
Classism was invented to uphold capitalism.

And so long as the oppressed cannot see
that their alleged "inferiority"
is an *invention*;
they too
will continue
to uphold oppression.

1610.

I am a Brown woman.

But who says I am?

The White man.

He labelled me as such
and I didn't get to say so much
and now I don't know who else I am.

***

How can we identify ourselves outside those colonial identities?
There is no space or language that is widely understood or accepted.

1611.

Growing up Brown
I knew my people were looked down
upon
by my teachers, who were White.
But they never taught me the language
to name how they didn't treat us right.
Instead they taught me they were right.
And when your feelings do not have any words
that you can call them, or name them,
you cannot communicate them
and thus you wonder whether they're real.

This is how White supremacy
is supposed to make you feel.

***

Like burger and fries,
White supremacy and patriarchal lies
have been fed to me
since childhood.

Until it became my favourite food.

Until it started to taste like common sense.
Until I forgot that I'm eating unhealthy pretence.

Until I remembered I need to *die*-t.
Until I realized starving is a riot.

1612.

English is not my mother tongue
but I am the daughter of an English colony.
And what moulds you isn't the womb
that you're born out of-
but the womb you are born into.

***

Colonial trauma also looks like
constantly apologizing
for your "broken English"
to colonizers
who will never apologize
for not only
not knowing a single word from your native language,
but for attempting to erase it.

1613.

I am not
what the White
man told you
about people like me.

I am not submissive
regressive
I am not a slave-
controlled by men
who can't behave.

I am me.
I am free.
Don't read the White man's narratives
his fantasy
his fetish
of oppressing
me.

Read about me
from me.

***

I am not your model minority
nor do I strive to be.

I have hell in my blood
and heaven in my ancestry.

You cannot build bridges
between the sky and the sea
to make an example
for the sands, out of me.

My body is not a fetish
to feast, your community.

My tongue is not exotic;
to my bone, it is the border
of my boundary.

My trauma does not lessen
when you use it as a lesson
on assimilation of diversity.

My joy will not be colonized
by your conditions of complicity.

Do not build a home
out of stereotypes, for me.

I am not a project
for you to project
your insecurity.

In this world I am only an 'other'
because you made yourself mother,
to force me to seek refugee
wondering about the roots

you buried under my family tree.

For I am home in my history
in my majority, I am no minority.
This world is not a model
moulded for your superiority.

I am not your model minority
nor do I strive to be.

1614.

I've been the only Brown academic
in rooms full of White.

They treated me as if I have borrowed this body
'cause I'm "*too smart* for Brown and *too bright*".

They discussed oppression and marginalization
and taught me what should and shouldn't be
my mother and my father's rights.

Yet something about those events
just didn't feel quite right,
especially when they expected me to quietly repeat
what *they* wanted to write.

I didn't have the language to explain
how those White academics
weaved White lies
or how I felt deeply in my Brown heart
that they don't actually give a damn.

Because in those White rooms
I was taught everything except White supremacy-
I only learned that from Brown activists on Instagram.

1615.

This is where we live now.

We moved in a few years ago,
the community was small
but it didn't take long to grow.

This is where we work now
where we talk
where we walk
where we play
where we pray.

This is where we *kind of* get to have a say-
where from the status quo,
we sway
away.

Our government is an algorithm
and violators don't give a damn.

This is where we live now;
welcome to Instagram.

***

Capitalism monopolizes on the spaces we are allowed to speak and
exist, so that it continues to have control over us.

Activist accounts are given space on social media, but also constantly censored and silenced- while hate speech is allowed to foster.

I am often asked: why do activists who complain about social media also still use it?

Marginalized folks fighting against the system often do not have the money or power to operate a platform that competes with existing social media platforms- so their choices are to either not share their work through such platforms that reach masses OR use the platforms to expose this system. They often choose the latter.

In an ideal world the exchange of knowledge should not be controlled by capitalism- but we don't live in an ideal world. And activists shouldn't be silent till then. That's why they're using social media despite complaining about it.

N.B. And that's why Elon Musk bought Twitter.

1616.

Instagram is not
sexist, racist, ableist, homophobic, and fat-phobic.

Instagram is merely a mirror.

It is a reflection of a world that is
sexist, racist, ableist, homophobic, and fat-phobic.

That is why whenever you report hate speech
they tell you "it doesn't go against our Community Guidelines".

How can we expect algorithms to have standards
against discrimination
when they were created by people that discriminate?

***

There are *men* behind
"Instagram's algorithm".

There are *men* behind
"violence against women".

To address a problem
without the clause,
is to change the problem
but keep the cause.

N.B. According to research developed by The Economist Intelligence Unit (and is supported by Jigsaw), 74% of the countries studied are failing to take appropriate corrective actions to address men's online violence against women. The result? Nearly **9 in 10** women restrict their online activity, limiting their access to employment, education, healthcare, and community. And **1 in 3** women think twice before posting any content online. (Source: "Measuring the prevalence of online violence against women", found online https://onlineviolencewomen.eiu.com/).

1617.

You don't notice
the *visible* White-washing in the media
because you're not supposed to.

It's supposed to be so visible
that it becomes invisible.

That's how Whiteness becomes default.

***

I find that on TV, in movies, in shows, in books, or even porn;
White, abled, heterosexual people are the default.

Everyone else is categorized under "minority" or "fetish".

Where do you fit?

1618.

We have doctors, and *female* doctors.
We have athletes, and *trans* athletes.
We have couples, and *gay* couples.
We have neighbours, and *Black* neighbours.
We have models, and *plus-size* models.
We have artists, and *disabled* artists.
We have a fault; but we call it "default".

***

Let's start saying
male doctors
cis athletes
heterosexual couples
White neighbours
minus-size models
abled artists...

N.B. They push us to the margins then call us marginalized!

1619.

Capitalism wants you to believe that Oprah Winfrey, Ellen DeGeneres (and other Hollywood celebrities who are from marginalized or LGBTQI+ communities) made it big because everyone has *equal access* to "beat the system" through hard work and perseverance.

That's not true at all.

For the majority of us, our hard work and perseverance will never pay off. Unless the heteronormative patriarchy allows some cracks to open up for us. And they do that sometimes. Not because they want to empower or reward our hard work- on the contrary- it's because they want to use us as the "model minority" and gaslight the rest of the marginalized and LGBTQI+ communities into the notion that *privilege doesn't exist.*

But if privilege doesn't exist there wouldn't be just one Oprah or one Ellen in Hollywood- there would be so many of them, the same way there are so many Harvey Weinstein's.

***

J.K. Rowling says she was rejected 12 times before a publisher accepted Harry Potter.

Have you ever thought of the fact
that if J.K. Rowling was Black
the world may have never known

Harry Potter?

But because she's White and cisgender
not only do we know Harry Potter,
but we also know she can be proudly transphobic
regardless of how this makes transgender lives suffer.

1620.

Male privilege also includes
denying male privilege.

White privilege also includes
denying White privilege.

Cishet privilege also includes
denying cishet privilege.

Privilege persists by
denying privilege.

***

You don't have to see your privilege to benefit from it.
But you have to see your privilege to dismantle it.

1621.

I am a woman.

I am a Brown woman.

I am a Brown, raised Muslim, woman.

My oppressions are visible.
They are the core of my disadvantaged identity.

I am also an abled woman.

I am also an abled heterosexual woman.

I am also an abled heterosexual, raised financially well-off, woman.

My privileges are invisible.
They are the status quo that I cannot deny benefits me.

***

My family are from the Shiite minority
in a land of Sunni majority;
our oppression is systemic
enforced in personal
and institutionalized levels,
my ancestors
lived in a struggle
to fight for me

though they never lived long enough to see,
but I know that every penny of privilege
I enjoy spending today
was once a prayer
of their blood and sweat
built for me to step
safely into every night and day.

My great grandfather died blind.
He started working when he was 12-
he worked too young and too hard
because the world wasn't too kind.

I am the daughter of oppression
whose ancestors defied this succession.

I will continue to use those privileges
that are keys of closed rooms
passed on like heirlooms,
to serve humanity
not just for the Shiite minority
but for all the women after me
even though, like my ancestors before me,
I won't be alive long enough to see-
it is progress when I help create a world
where my written words
are just history.

1622.

Self-care is a privilege,
so if you can afford it
use it for the greater good-
because if you don't take care of yourself
you cannot fully stand up
for those who are forced to sit down.

1623.

Having privilege
is not a bad thing
if you use your privilege
to do good things.

Having privilege
is not a bad thing
if you use your privilege
to stop the bad things.

Having privilege
is like having a candle lit
in total darkness.

When you use your light
to ignite
another candle's flame-
you don't lose anything, in fact you gain.

Because total darkness
becomes total lightness,
when we all light up the same.

***

Equality isn't a pie;
where if you give a slice to another
there will be less pie for you.

Equality is a candle;
where if you light up another
the entire path lights up for everyone.

1624.

What will happen to
envy
jealousy
greed
and oppression
if we truly know
that there is room for all of us?

This world had no walls.
Men built them.

1625.

"Taking freedom" from someone else
does not make you "more free";
it makes you an oppressor.

***

A woman doesn't have to be a feminist
for you to see that she is oppressed.

A man doesn't have to be a misogynist
for you to see that he has privilege.

You learn a lot about
the rights taken away from women
by observing the privileges given to men.

Behind every successful man
is a privilege afforded to him
at the expense of every woman.

1626.

"All men" doesn't mean all men are bad;
it means all men are *allowed* to be bad.

"All cops" doesn't mean all cops are bad;
it means all cops are *allowed* to be bad.

"All Whites" doesn't mean all Whites are bad;
it means all Whites are *allowed* to be bad.

And the fact that when you point out this systemic truth,
they normalize taking an aggressive stand;
is yet ironically another example of how
they're *allowed* to be bad.

1627.

For a White person having tanned skin
is a sign of the privilege of affording a summer vacation.

For a Brown person having tanned skin
is the cause of their oppression.

How wild is that?

***

Cultural appropriation is...

Brown skin seen as inferior
but when White folks tan they're *sun-kissed*.

Black hairstyles seen as unprofessional
but when White folks adopt them it's fashionable.

Africa seen as underdeveloped
but as a holiday destination it's exotic.

How are you participating in cultural appropriation?
We all do without noticing it.

1628.

The little Black girl
says she isn't beautiful
not because she isn't;
but because she understands
already
that beauty standards are determined
by White supremacy.

N.B. A video of a hairdresser comforting a little Black girl, who calls herself ugly, goes viral. See: https://www.today.com/style/hairdresser-comforts-little-girl-who-calls-herself-ugly-viral-video-t175703

1629.

How can you judge your beauty
by comparing it with someone else?
You're the only one
with this face and body.

How can you judge your success
by comparing it with someone else?
You're the only one
walking in your shoes
and on this journey.

Comparing is a colonial mindset
to make us uniform and erase our diversity.

Who is the benchmark?
Why did they set that standard?
How have you internalized it?

1630.

The professional appearance
required in the workplace
that erases all your individuality,
is because White supremacy ideals
have colonized your society.

N.B. Recommended reading: "The bias of 'professionalism'
standards" on Stanford Social Innovation Review (access
DOI: 10.48558/tdwc-4756).

1631.

We are taught to fear women
instead of fear the misogynists.

We are taught to fear homosexuals
instead of fear the homophobes.

We are taught to fear Black skin
instead of fear the racism.

We are taught to fear Jews
instead of fear the antisemitism.

We are taught to fear the marginalized,
by the oppressor who fears
being held accountable
for who they've victimized.

1632.

Systemic oppression
works in such a way
that it pushes you into oppression
and then at the same time
punishes you for falling.

It pushes Black folks into poverty
then creates laws that
punish them for committing crimes.

It pushes women into misogyny
then blames them
for being *too weak* across times.

You can't win
in a system
created to push you
and then punish you
for falling.

1633.

Oppressors tell you about Black-on-Black crime,
but they don't tell you about
how they pushed Black people into breeding grounds for crime.

Oppressors tell you gay men have a higher risk of HIV,
but they don't tell you about
how they didn't offer healthcare or sex education inclusive of the
needs of LGBTQI+ people.

Oppressors tell you women slut-shame, gossip, and backstab other
women,
but they don't tell you about
how they taught and normalized this behaviour in every movie and
story directed at girls from a very young age.

Be aware
of where
stereotypes come from.

Stereotypes do not come from the oppressed;
oppressors create the conditions to stereotype the oppressed.

***

Stereotypes dehumanize people
they make you infer about them
before hearing them.
They erase the voice of humans

they objectify humanity.

N.B. Intra-racial violence isn't specific to the Black community. But no one uses the phrase 'White-on-White' crime. Further reading: https://www.teenvogue.com/story/black-on-black-crime-myth

1634.

When I was in high school
my girlfriends and I
had a code word for our vaginas.

We called them 'Virginia'.

It was a combo of virgin and vagina and implies that we are talking
about a totally different State (pun intended) of affairs.

Meanwhile boys would say the words *pussy* and *cunt* without a care.

Thinking about it as an adult
I realize how many ways women code
their bodily parts and functions by default.

Vajayjay.
Down there.
Aunt Flo.
That time of the month.

The same shame
we are taught in hiding our body parts physically
is used to hide our body parts in discourse.

Who benefits from this of course
other than the men who continue to use our body parts as slurs?

***

"*Pussy*" is used to insult a man,
and "son of a *bitch*" is used to insult a man,
and every other word used to insult a man...
never uses "man" as an insult.

1635.

Don't use gay as an insult.
Don't use fat as an insult.
Don't use pussy as an insult.
Don't use Black as an insult.
Don't use crazy as an insult.

People- their sexualities, their bodies, their genitals, their skin colour, and their mental health- are not insults.

N.B. Recommended reading: "Why you need to stop using these words and phrases" on Harvard Business Review. Found online: https://hbr.org/2020/12/why-you-need-to-stop-using-these-words-and-phrases

1636.

"Don't be so crazy"
"This is insane"
"An eye for an eye makes the whole world blind"

Our language is ableist
and not at all kind.

***

The world is catered for the abled.

All the abled benefit
whether we realize it or not
everything is created for us
to see, hear, speak, and touch
and we move safely and freely
without thinking twice
because everything is catered
to our ability, and to enjoy life.

The same can be said
about the way all men benefit
from patriarchal systems
whether they realize or not
all men are treated as superior
while all women are not.

1637.

We tell women to be financially independent from men-
that this is the way to be free.

But what about women with disability?

Women who cannot work and have to rely on their spouse or family?

Can they be empowered while not being independent financially?
How will that look like?
Can we even imagine a possibility
where independence
doesn't have to involve money?

Our empowerment narrative is capitalist
and it is missing intersectionality.

***

Is there a way for us to compensate productivity
through a standard
that isn't for developed for the abled?

1638.

"Do you ever feel sad reading the news?"
I was asked.

"Don't we all?" I replied
"that's the point-
the news makes us feel sad
so that marketers can swoop in
with products and services
that promise to make us happy".

Capitalism would die
if the news made us happy.

1639.

They bombard you with advertisements
of stuff you don't need
then make you *pay more* for ad-free.

What a fucking joke.

You have to pay capitalism
to stop them from seducing you to pay
for stuff you don't need.

1640.

He's a broke broker.

I can tell from the broken screen on his phone
that never stops ringing
and his laptop tone
singing
whenever the market price goes up or down.
I see his face turn from smile to frown.

He comes every day
to the same secluded café,
where I sit to write
about patriarchy and oppression
and greed and capitalism,
and it's true what I make
barely pays my bills
because full-time independent *Brown* women authors
don't print books in gold mills...
But he makes me remember how miserable I'll be
if I lived life chasing after big buck money
so that one day I can live my life,
except when that day comes
there won't be much to live for.

I wish I can tell him to go find his passion
because life isn't about anything more.

***

Productivity is a product of capitalism;
you're valuable in being,
not in being valuable.

1641.

Is it not work, too,
to rest?

Lying down
to pick yourself up
when you don't feel your best?

To read a book
or two
window shop for new shoes online
watch TV
freely spend your time
to be free
go to the spa
take a nap
take no crap
take a crap
take a walk
bake a cake
have a break.

All this is a type of work
but it isn't seen as "work"
because it only serves *you*.

Capitalism defines work
as serving *others* with what you do.

***

The idea of a fixed weekend is capitalist.

Your rest days/ when you need rest can be different each week and depend on your level of energy and productivity.

Not everyone needs the same two days at the end of a week- and perpetrating that is part of the capitalist cycle that treats human labour as if they are standardized machines.

1642.

I got angry at the food delivery guy
for delivering my food while admitting
he has COVID.

Then I realized I should be angry at the restaurant
for working him to death.

When workers are punished for taking leaves,
they won't leave.

***

Nobody wants to work waiting on tables
but everybody wants to eat at restaurants.

***

"But it's not my fault that employers pay waiters minimum wage-
why must I be burdened with tipping?"
he said.

"Because" I told him "you're the one that's sitting
there buying a meal,
you're the demand to the supply in this deal,
you're the reason the restaurant keeps existing!
You contribute to the problem with a weekly devotion.
So why should you be exempt from the solution?"

1643.

The reason why we aren't taught
how to manage our own money in school
is because schools are products of oppressive capitalist structures.

They want us to learn
how to become employees
not investors.

***

Capitalism pays labour *just enough*
but *not enough*.

And by that I mean *just enough*
to feed themselves (to ensure they stay alive so that they can keep
coming to work),
but *not enough*
to have any wild dreams of independence from their employer like
owning property or starting their own business.

Just enough but *not enough* is a tactic
to protect the capitalist status quo.

1644.

Being able to afford
rent
childcare
domestic house worker
laundry service
or takeout food,
does not mean
you are *independent*.

It means you are privileged.

You cannot be independent
without some sort of privilege.

***

"Money can't buy happiness"
is something said by people
who think they can try buying everything (including happiness).

Money can't buy happiness- because some things in life aren't up for
sale. But that doesn't mean money isn't necessary. People don't just
want happiness; they also want food, shelter, and clothing.

Money can't buy happiness- but it can buy food, shelter, and clothing.

Money can't buy happiness- but it can pay the bills.

1645.

Time is money
only
for the rich.

For the poor
time is
debt.

***

Give a man a fish,
and he'll give it to a woman
to cook it for him to eat…

Teach a man how to fish,
and he'll hire employees
to go fishing on his behalf for minimum wage…

1646.

A dress
that sells
for $20
probably costs
around $10-$15 dollars to make.
That cost includes design, raw materials, electricity, salaries
and whatever else it takes.

But who pays for the cost
of the blood that drips
from the labour's fingertips
at the sweatshop...
sewing like playing
a grand piano
with your fingers trapped
under the piano lid cover?

Who pays for how much
those souls suffer?

Who pays for the voices lost in the humming
of the sewing
machine songs?
For the back strain and pain
from withstanding
to stay sitting for so long?

Who pays for the children abandoned
hungry
waiting at home,
yearning

for a mother that patriarchy owns?

Who pays for the years
of extremely underpaid labour
that are forever lost?

Do you ever think how much
a $20 dress
actually costs?

N.B. So many popular brands we consume and love use sweatshops to produce their products. Do your research before you buy. Every dollar you spend is a vote towards the kind of world you want.

1647.

Behind every great man
is a woman's greatly
unpaid and unequally paid
labour.

                              ***

It is more beneficial for capitalism to pay women less,
thus push them back into the homes
to perform free labour.

It is more beneficial for capitalism to pay low wages,
thus push people into taking loans
to owe the rich money.

It is more beneficial for capitalism when you're
dependent and in debt.

The rich make you poorer-
they take power;
and oppression is what you get.

1648.

I am not asking you to pay me equally to man.

I am asking why you think I shouldn't be paid equally to man?

***

Ask them
why they think
women should be paid less than men
for doing the same work.

And then listen to the misogyny unravel.

Because the only reason
women are paid less than men
is misogyny.

N.B. Actually, are they "paying women less" or are they *stealing portions of our income and thus making us work for free*? Language matters.

1649.

How much of women's already unequal pay
are we being conditioned to "pay back"
into patriarchy and capitalism?

***

Women are expected to *look* pretty
but never *feel* pretty enough.

Because this is how our appearance serves patriarchy,
but we still think we need to buy more
of the "improve your looks" stuff.

Our insecurities are manufactured.

They stereotype us saying "women love shopping" -
but they don't say it's because misogyny
is the greatest capitalist venture.

1650.

All of women's insecurities are manufactured by oppressors.

Our insecurities wouldn't exist without the tandem effort of racism, sizeism, and patriarchy- those systems create our problems for capitalism to sell us solutions.

Racism creates beauty standards based on White ideals.
Sizeism creates body standards based on thin ideals.
Patriarchy creates currency out of our bodies.

Then when you successfully feel that you aren't pretty enough, thin enough, good enough- capitalism sells you makeup, skin Whitening, cosmetic surgery, diet products, fashion, and more.

N.B. If cosmetic companies told you that you're beautiful the way you are, they would sell nothing.

1651.

No **woman's** magazine
ever taught us anything about **women**.

From beauty tips
to cooking recipes
to what to wear
to how to be pleasant
to sex tips-
they taught us only how to serve men.

***

The media focuses so much on women's bodies
and what women wear
because women are objectified.
There is a preoccupation and an obsession
with what women *look* like
as opposed to how we *feel, think*, and what we have to *say*.

1652.

Capitalism uses a woman's body
to sell everything *to men*
(from food to cars to sex).

But what does it use a woman's body
to sell *to women*
other than shame, insecurities, and unrealistic beauty standards?

***

Advertising
uses a woman's body
in marketing for men
to sell products *that elevate standards of living*,
but uses it for women
to sell products *that emulate living in patriarchy*.

1653.

Capitalism has turned biology against women.

We aren't allowed to age
to have stretch marks
or wrinkles
or to gain weight
or cellulite.
Our periods are soaked in pads
our pubes are sucked by razors.

We are expected to erase any signs of biology,
because patriarchy wants to treats us as inanimate objects-
and capitalism is here to serve patriarchy.

**

In the patriarchy,
to pass as a woman
one must look and behave like a girl.

We internalize this through rituals
like shaving our bodies,
eradicating our sexual desires,
downplaying our intelligence so as not to intimidate, etc.

If you do otherwise,
you're shamed or told you're not "womanly" enough.

How fucked up is that?

How fucked up is it that to be a "woman"
you're supposed to pretend you're still a "girl"?

1654.

Shaming women for aging doesn't stop them from aging-
it stops them from *feeling good* about aging.

When you stop them from feeling good,
you can easily invent insecurities for them.

Dye your white hair!
Get Botox for your wrinkles!

And they'll buy those products because they want to buy *hope*-
hope that if they obey, the system will give them the validation they
need to feel good about themselves again.

But that hope is an illusion- it is created by capitalism to get women
to keep on spending more *in hopes* of buying *hope*.

The system that profits from creating our insecurities
will never give us validation.

***

I am not dyeing
my grey hair
because it shows I haven't yet died.
Shaming women for aging
is shaming them for being alive.

1655.

Do y'all realize how many ways women are shamed
for NOT DYING?!

We're shamed for getting older.
We're shamed for having c-sections.
We're shamed for surviving assault.

When our mere existence
is defiance to a system
that wants our lives missing,
we dismantle the patriarchy
each time we choose living.

***

I didn't realize getting older was shameful
until I noticed women are taught to dread their birthdays
and it's a taboo for us to say how old we are.

I'm 35 and I'm living.

I didn't realize c-section shaming was a thing
until a male relative told me I took the "easy way out"
after a medically necessary c-section in which if I chose otherwise I
could have died.

I gave birth and I'm living.

I didn't realize being a survivor of assault
was more shameful than dying from it
until I was told I must bury what had happened into the grave of
silence.

I survived and I'm living.

I'm not dying while I'm living.

I'm living while I'm living.

When our existence threatens the patriarchy,
we dismantle the system each time we choose living.

So keep fucking living!

1656.

They keep us busy
worrying about our looks
so that we don't look
at how they're fucking up our world!

***

The older wicked women in the fairytales
are only wicked because they stopped tolerating bullshit.

Snow White's stepmother is wicked
for not fitting into beauty ideals,
and Ursula is wicked
for wanting to have power.

And not so coincidently,
neither of them are presented as lovable.

***

We're *victimized* when we're younger
and *vilified* when we're older.

We're catcalled, groped, harassed, and assaulted
way before we understand what all this violence means.

We spend a lifetime conflicted
between how wrong it feels to us
and how normalized it is by society.

And when we're finally old enough
to understand the scope of the trauma
and empowered to hold men accountable,
we are vilified as old miserable crazy witches.

N.B. They call you wicked when you call out their wickedness.

1657.

Womanhood is a
pain and *performance*
for the *pleasure* of patriarchy.

Pain of oppression;
of virginity myths, of periods,
of childbirth, of menopause,
of high heels, of corsets, of cosmetic surgery…

And a *performance*
of all of the above
without showing the *pain-*
because that's how we *please* the patriarchy.

***

Are you happy single?
They'll tell you *you're not.*

Feel pain wearing high heels?
They'll you *that's hot.*

Fuck this world forcing us to question
our common sense and logic
because they want us to normalize oppression.

1658.

Feel ashamed of your period
but aspire to have children.

Have children
but aspire for a career.

Aspire for a career
but prioritize your family.

Prioritize your family
but 'have it all'.

'Have it all'
but change who you are.

Change who you are
but don't change the world.

And women continue screaming
inside a cycle
that no one else heard.

                              ***

To become a woman
is to become everything
a man
would be shamed for...

1659.

Women are expected
to be sexy, but not sexual
to do the housework, but not get paid
to be nice, but not get treated nicely
to give, but not take.
to forgive, but never make a mistake
(or else, we deserve to be oppressed).

Is this a fucking test?

Because we're setup to fail.

***

Hide your body, but be sexy.
Be sexy, but don't have sex.
Don't have sex, but give sex.
Give sex, but take consequence.
Take consequence, but don't say NO.
Don't say NO, but your silence is a YES.
If you're confused, then you understand
what it means to be oppressed.

1660.

They want us to be virgins,
but also well experienced in bed.

They want us to cover our nipples,
but also to show our cleavage.

They want us to wear makeup,
but also to look natural.

They want us to cook and clean,
but also to not consider it labour.

They want us to live in a State Of Contradiction,
but also to never call it gaslighting.

***

Be sexy, but don't be sexual.
Not all men, but be wary of all men.
You need a man, but don't be a gold-digger.
Have a career, but pick family.
Be a woman, but you'll be treated like a girl.
And you're crazy if you think this is crazy.

Come on, it's so easy!

Be sexy. But don't be sexual.
Be skinny. But have a big butt.
Follow beauty standards. But don't enjoy the attention.
Study. But work at home.
Want kids? Go get married.
Abusive partner? Stay for the kids.

Now repeat after me:
I have it all.
I am free.

1661.

The suspected witch was tied and thrown in the river.

If she floats- she's a witch, thus executed.
If she sinks- she's innocent, but she dies.

So you see?
What can we learn from our history?

***

And nothing you do
is ever acceptable in the end,
because that's how
they ensure
the cycle of control
doesn't end.

1662.

The reason women are fed contradictions-
told to shut up but smile,
shave their bodies bare but then cover them up,
have thigh gaps but thick thighs,
stay safe but earn protection,
feel ashamed of their periods but aspire to have children-
is to ensure that there is always something women must change
about themselves
to distract us from realizing what needs to change is the world.

1663.

Being a woman
is a constant fighting of a war
between who the world wants you to be
and who you really are.

***

Their shame was never meant to find home
in your body.

Stop welcoming it.
Show it the door.

And ashamed you will be
no more.

***

In one lifetime,
a woman can be born
twice;
first into gender,
and second, out of it.

How many times were you born?

1664.

There's a reason they tell women to sacrifice for love
and that "self-love is selfish".

When you love yourself,
it is very difficult for oppressors to convince you otherwise.

Capitalism will struggle to sell you ways to improve yourself.
Patriarchy will struggle to get you to lower your standards for men.
Self-love means you win, and women aren't expected to win.
That's why they call self-love selfish.

So love yourself so fiercely
in all the ways
that this world tells you that you can't.

Because you can.

You really can.

1665.

Do you realize how many oppressive structures
will crumble down
if women were taught to love *themselves*?

Or, to put this differently,
do you realize how many oppressive structures
thrive
because they rely on teaching women
to hate themselves, feel insecure, inferior, and accept abuse?

Patriarchy, capitalism, religion, marriage, and politics,
are just to name a few.

A woman who loves herself first fiercely, and accepts nothing less,
is a terrifically terrifying being.

She is a revolt, and a revolution-
an individual, that is changing the collective.

In a world that profits out of inventing
women's insecurities, shame, pain, and sin;
self-love is radical activism.

1666.

Patriarchy invents women's insecurities.
Capitalism profits out of selling us solutions.

Patriarchy uses misogyny to create the idea that you aren't good
enough.
Capitalism sells you wrinkle cream, diet products, and cosmetics.

Patriarchy and capitalism work with one another against you.
So you need to work with yourself against them.

Self-love, self-acceptance, and self-healing are radical activism.

***

Self love is not selfish-
people who cannot love themselves cannot heal,
and when we don't heal
our wounds bleed into the world
creating a massacre.

1667.

Real women
don't have curves.

Real women
don't have thigh gaps.

Real women
don't have to be defined
by their bodies.

All women are real women.
All women have real bodies.

1668.

I look into the mirror
at the woman looking back at me.

She no longer sees the jury
and she is no longer a judge.

She doesn't say things like
"that isn't enough" or "that is too much".

I look into the mirror
at the woman looking back at me.
And I wonder
who is she?

She seems to now accept me totally.

She looks at the wrinkles I wear
sprinkled at the edges of my eyes.
She looks at the mountains
that I now call my thighs.

She sees the beauty of my truth
and the hideousness of patriarchy's lies.

I gained so much weight
in pounds and pounds of happiness.
I now feel so fulfilled of self-love and acceptance.

I dropped so much weight
in pounds and pounds of shame.
I no longer feel heavy when people call me

slut or whore or whatever other name.

I look into the mirror
at the woman looking back at me
she has changed from what I used to see.

Or maybe that's who she always was
but now I allowed her to be.

Free.

N.B. Change isn't always something new. It could also be allowing
ourselves to see what was always there.

1669.

You're too fat, or you're too thin;
'cause they don't want to let you win.

You're too quiet, or you're too loud;
'cause they don't want you to make a sound.

You're too giving, or you're too selfish;
'cause they don't want to see you flourish.

You're too slutty, or you're too prude;
'cause they don't want your attitude.

They're making you play a losing game
'cause they don't want your real stuff.

You're never too much, or too little
'cause you're *you*- and that's enough.

1670.

Stripping women from their bodies
is a cruel act of patriarchy.

Brain or boobs?
Sexy or smart?
Body or personality?

Which do you want to have?

When women's bodies are objectified,
we will choose our brains.
And then we realize patriarchy punishes our bodies
and also punishes our brains.

***

Young girls need to have role models
that are both sexy and smart- and not either/or.

We need to be able to see
that our beauty doesn't exclude our brains,
and our brains don't exclude our beauty.

We need to stop treating women as binaries.
We need to stop butchering women's full capacity.

1671.

We're taught that
beautiful girls shouldn't be angry
and angry girls aren't beautiful.

We're taught that
good girls shouldn't be sexual
and sexual girls aren't good.

We're taught that
we exist on a binary,
that only men have the right
to the full spectrum of humanity.

***

If you're sexy, then you're not smart.
And if you're smart, you can't be sexy.

If you're sexual, then you're not pure.
And if you're pure, you can't be sexual.

If you focus on your family, then you're not ambitious.
And if you're ambitious, you can't focus on your family.

If you're a feminist, then you hate men.
And if you love men, you can't be a feminist.

If you view women as a binary, then you aren't seeing their full

humanity.
And if you can't see women's full humanity, you can't get rid of the binary.

1672.

If we fight for equality in a patriarchy,
we're man-haters.
If we play along with patriarchy,
we're weak at best and manipulative bitches at worst.

This is because whether we fight within it or go along with it-
we are still inside the walls of patriarchy.
We are still judged by the standards of patriarchy.
There is no way for women out of patriarchy,
until there is no more patriarchy.

***

To be sexy is not respectable
and to be respectable is not sexy
and the only way to be both at the same time
is by viewing yourself outside the male gaze and its confine.

1673.

Brains OR boobs?!

I have a better question;
Why must I be forced to pick which parts of myself to embrace,
because you have been taught that you cannot value the 'whole' of a
woman?

Brains OR boobs?!

I have a better answer:
Fuck your binary.

***

She doesn't have to cover her body
for you to see her brain.
You have to cover your misogyny
for you to see her humanity.
Woman is not a binary;
she doesn't have to sacrifice any part of herself
just because you're taught to view her
as either/or, virgin/whore;
she is both, she is neither, she is more.

1674.

The liberation of women must include
the freedom *for* being sexual
AND the freedom *from* being sexualized.

It's not an either/or- we need both.

Freedom *for* being sexual
means I get to set the terms for my desires, whether I'm sexual or not,
who and how I fuck, what I wear, what I do with my womb, my rights
to consent and to orgasms.

Freedom *from* being sexualized
means all the aforementioned isn't dictated to me by men.

***

I am much more than my body.

But I also have a body.

A body that deserves the same respect
you're considering to give to my brain.
A body that doesn't want to be told
to conceal or reveal or feel shame.

Women are much more than bodies;
we are stardust and souls and goals and sighs and laughs.

But how can you respect women at all,
when you don't respect the bodies we have?

1675.

When you tell women to cover up their bodies to gain respect,
you are saying that respecting women is conditional.

And if respect relies on being conditional,
when a condition is fulfilled, a new one is invented.

That is why when a woman is already fully covered and *still* not
respected- she is told it's because she needs to do XYZ, and even
after XYZ she is still not respected.

When respecting women is conditional
women are never respected-
instead they are *expected*
to submit to never-ending conditions.

1676.

Isn't it ironic that
men say they objectify women
only because women objectify themselves
and yet anything we do
is considered objectifying ourselves
because men objectify everything we do?!

***

The thing is, under the laws of sex objectification,
you will be sexually objectified
whether you are dancing or doing the dishes.
So the solution isn't for women to stop dancing or doing the dishes.
Because even if women sit idle-
men will still find a way to sexualize that.

Being sexually objectified is a very specific way
of dehumanizing women no matter what they do.

That's why it's not under women's control and not their fault.

We have a right be sexual-
and just because we are sexually objectified
doesn't mean we have no right to be sexual
or that being sexually objectified is our fault for being sexual.

Because no matter what we do, under the laws of sex objectification,
we will still be sexually objectified.

When women's bodies are sexually objectified
it doesn't matter what we wear, what we do, or where we go -
we will still be seen as sex objects.

1677.

Women never had to do anything to be sexually objectified.

As soon as we're born
we're wrapped in pink, and tutu skirts, and hair bows-
making us look cute, training us to ignore how uncomfortable and
itchy we feel.

Next we have training bras and high heels -
even if we don't have any breasts or desire for sex appeal.

And then we have a range of modest to revealing clothes,
and whatever we wear is political and coded.

We must wear shorts for sports,
but must cover our shoulders for school.

And if we dare make a choice-
we're told we're brainwashed and *objectifying ourselves*.

1678.

You don't end your sexualization when you stop being sexual.

Women aren't sexualized for **being** *sexual*,
they are sexualized for **being**.

So stop apologizing for being sexual,
in a world that has yet to apologize
for sexualizing your existence.

Your sexualization doesn't end when you stop being sexual.
Your sexualization ends when men stop sexualizing you.

1679.

I was 11
the first time I was sexually harassed
by two strange older men.

They told me to wear a bra because they can see my nipples,
before bursting off into ripples
of laughter.

The way I saw my chest changed forever right after.

That day I bought not one
but two
bras to
wear on top of one another;
because I wanted to make sure
I wouldn't have to endure
or suffer,
through any of that humiliation again.

But of course it happened again and again.
By not only one or two
but by so many men.

I began to notice how they glare
at my breasts
when they talk to me
where their eyes would rest
as if they can see through my clothes
as if I wasn't dressed

despite the fact that I had 2 bras on
so I began
to wear three
and then four
and then more
and I still got the same looks
suffocating under eight bra hooks
until I was sore
until I couldn't breathe anymore.
It didn't occur to me
that no matter how many,
bras I wore
my breasts will always be,
naked in the eyes of men.

I was being objectified before I knew what objectification was;
I was a girl in the body of a woman.
I was only 11.

***

To constantly assume women's bodies are "asking for it" (while our
bodies aren't constantly asking for anything other than oxygen) is to
deny us from the basic humanity of existing beyond your erection.

Let us fucking live.

1680.

A girl's education can be disrupted
if her body is seen as a distraction.

A boy's education can't be disrupted
if his misogyny is causing a distraction.

They frown upon women's *lack of modesty*
but say nothing about men's *excessive misogyny*…

***

People shame women
for showing skin
instead of shame men
for objectifying women;
without realizing that
they wouldn't see the former offensive
if the latter wasn't pervasive.

People shame women
for being feminists
instead of shame men
for being misogynists;
without realizing that

they wouldn't see the former offensive
if the latter wasn't pervasive.

1681.

How can modest *clothes*
be considered a solution
to prevent/ end the sexualization of women,
when the problem isn't whether the *clothes* are sexualized,
but that the *bodies* underneath them always are?!

We expect a woman to cover her body
to end her objectification.
But the problem isn't her body-
it's patriarchy!

It is not the mini-skirt that objectifies,
but misogyny.

The mini-skirt cannot objectify a body
that isn't *already* objectified.

And if we keep blaming it on her clothes,
we will never see the cause

                    ***

The only way a short dress
can cause the objectification of a woman
is if it was worn around a body that is already objectified.

And the only way a hijab
can end the objectification of a woman
is if it was wrapped around the eyes objectifying her.

1682.

"Stop objectifying women"
doesn't mean tell women to cover their bodies-
because that is objectification too.
"Stop objectifying women"
means stop telling women what to do!

Instead of telling your daughter
to cover up
because her uncle is coming over,
how about you tell her uncle
that your daughter isn't a sex object?

Instead of telling girls to cover up their bodies at school,
how about you tell boys that girls aren't sex tools?

Instead of telling girls and women to cover up their bodies,
how about you tell men to cover up their misogyny?!

***

You know what?
I wish baggy clothes could protect us.

I wish it was that simple.

I wish all I need to do
is put on some sweatpants
and be safe from sexual assault.

But it doesn't work that way.

You know why?

Because women are not given access
to protective shields in the patriarchy.

So stop telling us to change our clothes
and start changing the system!

N.B. It doesn't matter what women wear/ do/ go- if men are taught to view them as objects, women can't change that by simply changing their clothes or direction.

1683.

He tells her while upset;
put on a longer skirt-
your body is too revealed
I can't *allow my girl* to go out like that.

She asks him to reflect;
is the problem my short skirt-
or what you're taught about your masculinity
and how to perform it?

***

When you teach a girl or woman
that if she changes her clothes
she can end her oppression,
you are teaching her
that *her clothes are the cause* of her oppression.

You are teaching her that *her actions* can end her oppression.

And if you teach her that her actions can end her oppression,
you also teach that her actions *cause* her oppression.

This is victim blaming.

***

When a woman is shamed for revealing her body,
she is being forced to cover it.

When a woman is shamed for covering her body,
she is being forced to reveal it.

And whenever women are forced to battle with their bodies,
the only winner is patriarchy.

1684.

 "Let's ban the hijab!" she screamed
"no more symbols of patriarchy!"

But you see,
under your logic,
let's ban marriage then...
let's ban removing body hair...
let's ban high heels...
why draw the line at the hijab?
All of those things are patriarchal.
If you want to ban certain things and not others,
you need to reflect on your internalized colonial bias.

The solution isn't to ban individual people from choosing for their
own bodies and lives- by doing so you take away their freedom which
makes you the same as the oppressor. The solution is to ban systems
from conditioning people on what to choose.

***

When you discriminate against a woman wearing hijab-
you blame her for a system invented by men.
You hold women accountable for misogyny
while you let the misogynists run free!

1685.

Saying:
wearing religious symbols publically is banned
so why should we make an exception for hijab?

Is like saying:
showing underwear publically is indecent
so why should we make an exception for bra straps?

***

"But other religious people don't make a fuss about being told not to
wear religious symbols...so why should we give an exception to
women with hijab?" they say.

Perhaps the issue here is that there is no way to properly compare the
hijab with other religious symbols because no other symbols are
required to be worn in the same way.

Perhaps comparing is our way of neatly categorizing the world, but it
also erases our diversity, and makes us sit inside the boxes built for us
by colonizers.

Perhaps we shouldn't compare.
Perhaps we should let people be.
Perhaps instead of learning how to compare,
we need to learn about diversity.

1686.

If you fight against forcing women to *take off* hijab,
but you don't equally fight against forcing women to *wear it*;
then you're not fighting for women-
you're fighting for systems that oppress women.

Because women pay the price.

Women pay the price when modesty is *denied*
and women pay the price when modesty is *forced*.

And until we see that women are always paying the price- we will
keep on fighting for the beliefs of men that end up killing women.

****

And I think it is possible to find that spot where we counter hijab and
question the system while also making sure we don't harm the women
who wear it.

I don't feel comfortable holding women accountable for what
patriarchy has imposed on us- it is victim blaming.

We (who have the privilege/ awareness to unlearn) should direct our
anger at the system/ structure not at the women who are victims of it-
otherwise we inadvertently reproduce the cycle of misogyny.

N.B. A Congress MLA in Karnataka said "rape rates are highest in India because several women don't wear hijab" amid protests regarding schools banning hijabs in India. Found online: https://www.ndtv.com/karnataka-news/rapes-because-women-dont-wear-hijab-karnataka-congress-mlas-shocker-2766492

1687.

Is hijab a choice?

There is a difference between
being *taught* to choose something
and being *forced* to choose it.

The former can feel like a choice
but neither are *choices*.

It is not a choice if you're taught to choose it.
It is not a choice if you're shamed when you choose otherwise.

Under patriarchy nothing is a choice for women
whether it's hijab or high heels or makeup or grooming or or...
we are either taught to choose or forced to choose.

It is not a choice if the options are structured to prioritize the comfort
of men. For women to have a choice, our options shouldn't exist in
relation to men's approval.

***

"You can choose a different way" they say.

No I can't.

When the choices have been chosen for me.
When every choice is filled with oppression.
I cannot simply "choose" my way to freedom.

1688.

Modesty is not a choice.
Marriage is not a choice.
Motherhood is not a choice.

You may choose those things,
but would you have chosen them
if you weren't taught or forced to?

We will never know.
That's something the patriarchy robs from us.

We certainly may choose those things.
But we will never know whether we chose them
because we want to
or because we're conditioned to.

Would we choose modesty
if we weren't shamed for revealing our bodies?

Would we choose marriage
if we weren't shamed for being single?

Would we choose motherhood
if we weren't shamed for being childfree?

No one knows.

We often hear "let women choose!",

but we don't often question "how do women choose?"

And then we perpetuate the cycle of misogyny
by shaming women for choosing (they are weak, brainwashed,
submissive if they don't make the "right" choice- whatever that is)
but we don't hold the patriarchy accountable.

Would we shame women,
 if patriarchy didn't teach us to never blame the oppressor?

***

No one has to tell you to wear a hijab,
they just call you a sinner if you don't-
and then, by yourself, you'll wear a hijab

No one has to tell you to save your virginity,
they just call you a slut if you don't-
and then, by yourself, you'll save your virginity.

No one has to tell you to get married,
they just call you a spinster if you don't-
and, by yourself, you'll get married.

No one has to tell you not to get an abortion,
they just call you a murderer if you do-
and then, by yourself, you'll stay pregnant.

No one has to tell you not to be a feminist,
they just call you a nasty, bitch, man-hater if you are-
and then, by yourself, you'll accept patriarchy.

No one will tell you that women don't have a choice,
they just shame the alternatives-
and then, by ourselves we'll pick what they chose for us.

Democracies proudly boast about not regulating women,
but they shame them-
and then, by ourselves, we self-regulate.

N.B. Patriarchy works better not when it regulates women but when it
teaches them to self-regulate.

1689.

Do not ban individuals from choosing.
Ban systems from conditioning.

It's easier to pick on individuals
than a collective belief system
that conditions our reality.

But it's not the right thing to do.

The truth is, under patriarchy,
women don't have the power to make free choices-
if we did, we would have "chosen" not to have a patriarchy.

***

Dear Men,
telling her she doesn't need makeup to look pretty, is the same as
telling her she needs makeup to look pretty
telling her she doesn't need to cover her body, is the same as
telling her she needs to cover her body
telling her she doesn't need to do something, is the same as
telling her she needs to do something.
Because in both cases, there is someone *telling* her what to do.
You're not *saving* her from any patriarchal standard- you're
telling her what to do, and in doing so reproducing patriarchal
standards.

Why not *listen* to what she wants and then act accordingly?

Instead of *telling* her what to do constantly....

When we're fighting those patriarchal standards it's important to remember that we are fighting the system for *normalizing* those things and not fighting the individuals for *internalizing* those things (this is victim blaming).

***

When I fight patriarchy
I fight systems
not victims.

I fight systems
for *normalizing* patriarchal standards,
I don't fight individuals for *internalizing*
those standards.

Fight the system;
speak out against the laws
the government
the media
the marketing
the religion.

You can't warn people that they're on fire
when the system has taught them
that hell feels like home.

1690.

Feminism, at its core, is an ideology
that empowers women to "opt out".

Whether from marriage, pregnancy, motherhood, staying at home-
women need to realize they are allowed to opt out from roles the
patriarchy forces us to take.

So the men who tell you "feminism hates men" are also telling you
that women opting out from roles that serve men is a form of hate on
men instead of realizing forcing women to take those roles is
misogyny...

Absurdly, men become victims when they aren't allowed to victimize
women.

***

Dear Sister,

No one is taking you to hell
for not wearing a hijab
for having sex outside marriage
for having an abortion.

Hell is
being denied your basic human rights
to decide whether or not you want to do those things.

Hell is patriarchy.

Hell is here. We live in it.

1691.

Empowerment in terms of clothing is contextual.

So if I grew up in a society that forces me to reveal my body,
I would feel empowered defying that message.

And if I grew up in a society that forces me to conceal my body,
I would feel empowered defying that message.

It is not about rebellion- it is about dismantling the structure that
controls me and taking back my power to decide. That structure can
be anything from fashion to religion.

The ideal situation would be no structure forcing women to reveal/
conceal their bodies, the way there aren't any structures like that for
men. And it wouldn't matter whether a woman's clothing is revealed
or concealed the way it currently doesn't matter whether men's
clothing is revealed/ concealed.

***

They say
modesty is the right way
because you're not supposed to be attracting men...
But they also say
that men are attracted to women who embrace modesty...

So we're supposed to dress a certain way that doesn't attract men...

for us to be attractive to men?

Does this mean that no matter what women wear- they'll still be attractive to men?

Sooo...does this mean the problem isn't our clothes- but the way men look at us?!

1692.

Why don't you give us a smile?
You'll look beautiful that way.
Never mind
that I'm a strange man
who just expects you to do what I say.

Why don't you give us a smile?
You'll look beautiful that way.
Never mind
that I'm demanding more labour
on top of your unpaid and unequal pay.

Why don't you give us a smile?
You'll look beautiful that way.
Never mind
that it hasn't crossed my mind
you don't exist in this moment to please me today.

Why don't you give us a smile?
You'll look beautiful that way.
Never mind
that I'm the one making a big fuss
the actual problem is that you won't obey.

Why don't you give us a smile?
You'll look beautiful that way.
Never mind

that the patriarchy
hates you either way.

Why won't you give us a smile?!
I said you'll look beautiful that way!
Never mind
fuck you
you're an ugly bitch anyway!

***

Just because you're attracted to her-
doesn't mean you have the right to objectify her.

Just because you're attracted to her-
doesn't mean she wants to attract you.

Learn the difference.

1693.

They make love out of our bodies.
They make life out of our bodies.
They even make objects out of our bodies.
But they don't make *us* out of our bodies.

There is a *person* attached to the womb, the legs, the sex.
There is a *person* attached to the hips, the waist, the breasts.
When we forget the person, we treat them as organs...

***

A short skirt
isn't an invitation or even a probability,
because consent to sexual liberation
isn't consent to sexual activity.

1694.

Liberating women from sex objectification
doesn't happen by denying women's sexual agency.
It happens by denying men the agency to objectify women.

And this doesn't mean
denying men the agency to be attracted to women;
it means you can be attracted to a woman
while realizing she doesn't exist to attract you.

Sex objectification is the inability to view women
beyond sexual attraction.
You can be attracted to women without objectifying them.

The difference between sexual
objectification and *attraction*,
is whether you view a woman
through or *beyond*
your erection.

***

**Sexual Objectification vs. Sexual Attraction:
What's the difference?**

Sexual Objectification (harmful):
1) Reduction of a person to mere body parts, while treating the

person's worth as nothing more than 'sex'.
2) Results in disregard of consent, normalizes rape culture, and ignores the humanity of the person.
3) Reflects in the systemic overpowering, shaming, and legislating of the person's body parts within and outside of sex.

Sexual Attraction (healthy):
1) Recognition of an attraction to a person's body parts, while acknowledging that the person's worth isn't in 'sex'.
2) Results in respect, boundaries, and treats a person with human dignity.
3) Reinforces systemic accepting, valuing, and rewarding of the person's contributions within and outside of sex.

How can you make a difference?
*Be aware of how you have personally been conditioned and are complicit in upholding sexual objectification (we all internalize this from our environments).
*Consistently put the effort to stop viewing people through the lenses of sexual objectification.

1695.

If bra straps "distract men"-
how many bras do we need
to bring the downfall of patriarchy?

If a woman's body "distracts men"-
how many naked women would it take
to bring the downfall of patriarchy?

Answer: Zero.

The biggest scam of patriarchy
is re-branding victim blaming
as power over men.

                    ***

My mini-skirt isn't a threat or a trigger.

My clothes have no power
to overpower
the men in power.

If my mini-skirt had the power
to bring the downfall of men
there would be no patriarchy.

1696.

If a man is harassing a woman
it's because "*she's* putting it out there"
and if a man cheats with another women
it's because "*she's* a home wrecker".

Why do we always blame women for what men do to them?

Why do we continue to perpetuate the myth that men "lose control"
when it comes to sex?

This "boys will be boys" mentality stops us from unlearning
patriarchy.

Men are "in control" of literally everything, including the creation of
this myth that they are helpless when it comes to sex.

Men never lose control; they enact entitlement and ownership over
women's bodies and then when called out- they victim blame women
for seducing them. And it's been happening since Adam blamed Eve.

IF men can truly "lose control"- patriarchy would have never existed
or persisted to this day.

***

You tell women to cover their bodies
when what you actually want to do
is tell men to cover their eyes.

Why don't you say it as it is?

Women's sex appeal isn't responsible for men's thoughts,
because men's thoughts create women's sex appeal.

"Sexy" is in the eye of the beholder.
Do not blame women for what men see as sexy.

1697.

There is nothing sinister
about a woman's body.
All that is sinister
is inside the eyes
gazing at her.

***

He begs for your nude,
but once you send it you're a slut.

He begs to have sex with you,
but once you consent you're a slut.

Does he not see the irony?

The only thing that made you a slut
is proximity to *his* "eyes" and "body".

1698.

Is she too loose, or are you too small?
Is she too much, or are you too little?
Is she too loud, or are you struggling to silence her?

What you say about her
is a comparative reflection of you not her.

The sin is in your eyes
not in her body.
The disrespect is in your eyes
not in her body.
You are looking,
she is but a mirror.

When will you stop holding her accountable
for what you see in her?

***

She's a slut? What makes her a slut? Lots of dick?
So you shame her because *you* think dick is dirty?

She's a whore? What makes her a whore? Charges for sex?
So you shame her because *you* want sex for free?

She's a bitch? What makes her a bitch? Doesn't accept your bare
minimum?

So you shame her because *you* can't keep up with her?

Your misogyny reflects you, not her.

1699.

The shame is not in her body.

Not in the spread of her thighs.

Not in the dress she is wearing or the underwear she is taking off.

None of that matters.

The shame is not in her *body*,
it is in the *mind* that does not respect her.

***

YOU look at a woman
YOU think of sex
YOU blame her.

How is it HER fault?

Blaming a woman for her sexualization
is like blaming the mirror for looking at you.
What you see in her, is a reflection of you.

1700.

A woman in pantyhose is objectified.
Not because she's in pantyhose.
But because she's in a patriarchy.

A man in pants is not objectified.
Not because he's in pants.
But because he's in a patriarchy.

She is objectified not because of what she's wearing,
but because of how people are taught to see her.

He is not objectified not because of what he's wearing,
but because of how people are taught to see him.

Objectification is the reducing of a person to a body
and a reducing of a body to an object.
It has nothing to do with what you do,
but everything to do with how
people are taught to see you.

1701.

There are governments
that tell women what they can and cannot wear,
and courts that tell us what we can and cannot do with our wombs.
There are fathers and husbands
and myths and religions...
is this all a coincidence?

Patriarchy isn't a coincidence.

1702.

The reason why a man **can** safely be topless
in a room full of women,
isn't because women aren't sexual;
but because men aren't sexualized.

The reason why a woman **can't** safely be topless
in a room full of men,
isn't because men are sexual;
but because women are sexualized.

And the reason why women don't systemically rape men
the way they rape us
isn't because women aren't as sexual-
it's because men aren't sexualized.

***

"But men are sexualized too" they say.

No they aren't.

Sure men can be seen as sexual when they enact it (which means
they're still in control of how they're viewed). But being sexualized
means you are viewed as a sex object to be consumed by another
person's desire regardless of what you're doing- and this lens has
never been systemically used to view men, more specifically cishet
men.

No one controls what men can or cannot wear.

No one judges them for how much skin they hide or show.

No one thinks a topless man is "asking for it".

No one thinks a man's only value is in the "purity" of his body.

No one asks men what they were wearing when they report rape.

Men can be seen as sexy and/or sexual. Men can even be victims of sexual harassment. But men are not sexualized. Let's not confuse the terms.

To be sexualized requires a systemic and institutionalized perception of your gender as a sex object.

To be sexualized requires tradition, culture, religion, capitalism, laws and a myriad of structures that come together to treat you as a sex object; as body parts that are more valuable than the sum of you.

Men, especially cishet men, don't ever experience that.

***

Cishet men aren't sexualized.

Ask a cishet man how he feels being called "sexy" by a strange woman- most likely he'll tell you it's *flattering*.

Ask a woman how she feels being called "sexy" by a strange man- most likely she'll tell you it's *frightening*.

Cishet men aren't sexualized.

To be sexualised not only requires a systemic and institutionalised perception of your gender as a sex object, but also to instil that fear of dehumanisation in you.

1703.

A man wearing shorts
"oh, he's just *feeling* hot"
A woman wearing shorts
"oh *she's* hot"

His clothes are seen as an expression
of his human self.
Her clothes are seen as an extension
of her objectification.

***

Male nipples are sexual.
Female nipples are sexualized.
Male bodies are sexual
Female bodies are sexualized.

When you're seen as sexual
you don't get sexualized.
But when you're sexualized
you're not seen as sexual.

***

Women's nipples are censored
not because they're sexual,
but because they're sexualized.

Men's nipples are sexual too,
but why aren't they censored?

Women's bodies are subjugated to modesty
not because they're sexual,
but because they're sexualized.

Think about it; men's bodies are sexual too,
so why aren't they subjugated to the same standards of modesty?

"Sexual" is an expression.
"Sexualized" is the imposing of a sexual expression.

1704.

In the patriarchy, men have bodies that can be sexual.
But women are sexualized because they have bodies.

Men are seen as sexual
when they behave in a way that is sexually suggesting.
Women are sexualized
just for existing.

Men aren't seen as sexual
until they do something sexual.
Women are sexualized
even when they're not doing anything sexual.

When a woman reveals her body, it's immoral.
When a man reveals his body, it's normal.

Women's bodies are seen as limited to sexual functions.
Men's bodies are seen as functional beyond sex.

1705.

Is it seriously too much
to expect women
to be free and sexual
and free to be sexual?!

***

It is your RIGHT to be sexual,
they're WRONG to sexualize you.

Women have the right to exist however they want
and men have no right to objectify women.

To assume that the eradication of sexualization
is achieved by women not being sexual,
is to say that being sexual is THE CAUSE of sexualization.

It isn't.

THE CAUSE is patriarchy and how it views women.

Women have the human right to be sexual.
Men don't have the right to sexualize women.

1706.

"Women sexualize themselves" they say.

No we don't.

Women are *sexualized*.

Which means whatever we do
(whether it's sexual or not)
you'll still find a way to call it "hot".

Women are sexualized
whether we are in the bedroom
or the conference room.

There is a fetish for the stripper
and a fetish for the nun.

The virgin is defined *by sex*
and the whore is defined *by sex*.

So when you say "women sexualize themselves"
what you actually mean is
you don't want to take the blame for it.

You will continue to sexualize us anyway
no matter what we do,
but you just want us to blame ourselves for it.

We won't.

We won't *see* our sexuality with objection,

just because you *sow* our objectification.

***

And let it be known that
a woman expressing her sexual being
is NOT sexualizing herself,
she is *expressing* **just one part**
of the many parts of herself;
sexualizing is when you look at her
as a sex object, and nothing else.

1707.

Women are accused of "sexualizing themselves"
at the hint of showing any sexual agency.

Our sexual empowerment is married to shame.
Our pleasure is divorced from purity.
Those relationships are destructive;
they can never conceive women's sexual agency.

And they exist because
men aren't being blamed for sexualizing women;
but women are blamed for being sexualized by men.

And so women are accused of "sexualizing themselves"
because the world struggles
to imagine women being "sexual for themselves".

Our sexual narrative is broken, and breaking us.

Start unlearning.

There's no such thing as "women are sexualizing themselves";
there's either "women are blamed for being sexualized by men"
or "women are shamed for being sexual".

***

You cannot "sexualize yourself".
They use this language to confuse us into thinking

our sexual expression is somehow on par
with their sexualization of us.

You also cannot "un-sexualize yourself"
because you aren't the one sexualizing yourself.

When they say: Stop sexualizing yourself!
What they mean is: Stop expressing yourself as a being who is sexual
otherwise don't blame me for not seeing you beyond that!

Fuck them.

1708.

"She's just dressed like that for attention" he says with disapproval.

"So what?" I ask him.

What is so harmful about a woman wanting attention?
You are so used to erasing, belittling, reducing women-
until YOU want to give them attention.
And she has decided not to shrink
until you inflate her.
She's standing tall and you noticed that
and now you feel small.
You're pissed she didn't fold herself up in the corner
and wait for you to decide whether to acknowledge her or not.
You're triggered and it's *your* problem.

So what if a woman wears certain clothing for attention?
Is it a crime for women to want attention?

Last time I checked, when men want attention
no one is shaming them for it.

Women can, just like men,
wear clothes out of comfort and choice.
And women can, just like men,
wear clothes to sexually attract and seek attention.
All those reasons can exist and all of them are okay.

***

"Attention-seeker"
is an insult
only in a world that convinced you
that you don't deserve any attention.

1709.

We decide
what's sexy or modest or what isn't.

We decide
what's a "slut" and what's a "virgin"
to link "sex" with "sexual orientation"
and throw in gender identity.

We decide
what skin colour corresponds to supremacy.

We decide.
We decide.

We decide what to see.
We decide which one
is the *right* way to be.

There is no truth in this decision
or objective reality;
we decide to agree
we decide collectively.

Here's how we decide as a society;
Patriarchy
narrates misogynistic fiction
this tale has no power
until we feed it conviction;
we give it life
we make it non-fiction.
So in the same way that

we decide to learn
we can decide to unlearn-
we can decide to agree
we can decide collectively
to dismantle patriarchy.

***

Patriarchy has no power
besides **your power**;
i.e. the power you give it.

You can dismiss it.

1710.

Is she a slut,
or are you unable to comprehend
that women can enjoy sex the way men do?

Why is she a slut...
for doing the exact same thing
that if done to her by a man,
makes him a stud?

Are men never "slutty"?
Or are we taught to never view
their sexual expression as "slutty"?

***

Slut-shaming is a symptom
of a society that expects
sex
to take *something* away
from women.

Sex takes *nothing* away
from women.

***

A slut doesn't exist
except in the mind of a person
conditioned to believe
that a woman enjoying sex
the way men do
is somehow deviant.

1711.

The only difference between
a virgin and a whore
is not who they are fundamentally,
but the *perception* of who they are
assigned to them by patriarchy.

The shaming of a woman's sexual agency
isn't because of what she's doing,
it's because she's viewed through patriarchy.

***

I am neither a virgin nor a whore;
abolish the idea that women
are a social construction
of whether or how much
men score.

1712.

"Virgin" is expecting a woman to be valued…
for what men have yet to do to her body.

"Prude" is expecting a woman to be ashamed…
for not wanting men to have her body.

"Whore" is expecting a woman to be ashamed…
for profiting from what men have done to her body.

"Slut" is expecting a woman to be ashamed…
for enjoying what men have done to her body.

In the patriarchy women are blamed for everything
that men do or don't do to their bodies.

1713.

Virgins don't exist.
But misogyny does.

Sluts don't exist.
But misogyny does.

Spinsters don't exist.
But misogyny does.

Bitches don't exist.
But misogyny does.

The only reason
they label you
is because misogyny
taught them to.

***

If he shames you
using the virgin/ whore dichotomy,
accuse him of misandry.

Yes, *misandry*.

Because if absence of dick in a woman's body
makes her pure

and its presence in it
makes her impure-
then he's saying *dicks are dirty*.

Man-hater!

1714.

The slur *slut* has become a rite of passage.

When a girl hears it,
she knows she is now held with the accountability of a woman.
And when a woman hears it,
she knows she is now unaccounted for.

***

"You're a slut!" he says.

After we had premarital sex.
After he coerced me to say yes.

Now I'm a slut. Damaged goods
which basically means
(as he didn't explain, but I understood)
that I am someone who knows too much
about his predatory abusive insidious misogynistic ways.

Now he wants a girl who is "pure"
(a new victim), not a whore
to ensure
she isn't aware of what he
likes to do to girls
like what he just did to me
so that he can do it all over again
to her.

"You're a slut!" he says.

Which means I have emerged
fully aware
holding him accountable
for the math
of the aftermath of his mess.

"You're a slut" he says.

i.e. you know too much now,
let me move on to someone who isn't aware of
what I just did to you
so that I can do it to them and break them too.

***

If you claim it's *immoral* for women to enjoy their own bodies,
but *normal* for men to enjoy women's bodies-
then you're not concerned about *morality*,
you're concerned about *ownership*.

If you believe a woman *revealing* her body is immoral,
but a man *revelling* in her body isn't-
then your concern isn't about maintaining morality.
It is about perpetuating patriarchy.

1715.

They want nudes,
but shame you for sending them.

They want sex,
but shame you for fucking them.

They want sexual control,
so they shame you for consenting.

***

Sending a nude your boyfriend requested is sexy,
but selling your own nude is slutty.

Stripping for your boyfriend is sexy,
but being a stripper is slutty.

They'll have you believe that your sexual expression is shameful...
but only when you have ownership of it.

***

When women are shamed
for not consenting to sex (prude)
and also shamed for consenting to sex (slut)-
then we aren't shaming women for their sexual activity.

We're shaming them for *ownership* of their sexual activity.
We're shaming them for having a choice.

1716.

The shaming of a woman's sexual expression
has been branded under morality, purity, and religion-
but it is ownership and patriarchy.

The shaming of women's sexual expression
occurs in spaces where she demonstrates ownership of her sexuality.

If they cannot own you,
they will shame you instead.

It's the next best way to control you.

***

If they *force* you when you say "no"
and *shame* you when you say "yes"-
it's not that they don't understand your consent.

It's that they want you to associate
your consent with consequence.

Because that's how you're tricked into staying silent.
And your silence is required for their violence.

1717.

Perhaps women who don't "reveal their bodies"
avoid doing so
not because of feeling ashamed or shy
but because of a lack of safety.

Perhaps there are no *shy* women;
deep down we just know we aren't *safe* in our bodies.

***

Have you realized that
women on social media are censored
for HAVING bodies?

That is why when women post pictures of themselves-
they're sexualized by men.
But if women post *sexy* pictures of themselves-
they're banned by social media.

Our consent has no room,
when control is taking up all the space.

1718.

"Free the nipple" campaigns aren't trivial,
nudes on social media aren't vanity,
and consensual sex work isn't oppression.

All those things force you
to see the *agency* of the women doing them.

And when you see the agency of women,
you humanize them.
And when you humanize women,
you stop seeing them as sex objects.
And when you stop seeing women as sex objects,
you walk towards their liberation.

Because every oppression women experience
(from female genital mutilation, to safe abortion bans, to domestic
violence, to unequal pay, to sex trafficking, and more)
is due to the perception that we are, not humans with agency,
but sex objects.

1719.

Women should use their own bodies
however way they want
without being *shamed-*
men have been doing that to us
without being *ashamed.*

Why do they want us to be ashamed
for doing what they do without shame?!

***

They teach us that
stripping
from shame
is shameful....
but *what's shameful*
is that they teach us
that stripping
from shame
is shameful.

Break the cycle.

1720.

If revealing her body makes a woman so bad,
then why do men want to see her body so badly?

If having sex makes a woman so bad,
then why do men want to have sex with her so badly?

If using her body to profit makes a woman so bad,
then why do men use it to profit so proudly?

Ask yourself;
why are women considered so bad
for doing the things that are considered normal
for men to want so badly?

Shame is an invention of patriarchy;
it is invented to strip women from their own bodies
and gift those bodies to men.

***

Patriarchy: controls women's bodies.
Capitalism: uses women's bodies to sell.
Government: legislates women's bodies.
Religion: shames women's bodies.

Woman reclaims her body

Men: "Women, your worth is not in your body!" i.e. reclaiming your body makes it difficult for us to control, use, legislate, and shame your body.

1721.

Patriarchy wants women's bodies so badly.

Like so badly.

But the second we want our own bodies so badly too,
the second we embrace our bodies and exude confidence
and own our sexual desires without shame-
we're *fucking good for nothing sluts*.

Patriarchy wants women's bodies so badly,
but they don't want us to want our own bodies so badly too-
because how can they use and abuse our bodies
when we own our own bodies so badly?

1722.

Why is it that when men rap about women's pussies- it's art
but when women rap about their own pussies- it's shameful?

Why is it that when men put women in sexy clothes to sell products-
it's marketing
but when women wear sexy clothes to feel good- it's shameful?

Why is it that when men watch women violated in porn- it's kink
but when women make porn on their own terms or consent to kinks-
it's shameful?

Why are we lead to believe that women's sexual expression is
inherently shameful,
when clearly it is only women's *ownership* of their sexual expression
that's shamed?

***

When men rape women- it's their natural urge.
When women consent to sex- they're sluts.

When men watch porn- it's their natural urge.
When women consent to sex work- they're whores.

When men claim- it's normal.
When women reclaim- it's immoral.

This shame makes women recline.

But from now on I'll redirect all shame I was given, to the men-
they should be ashamed for taking what's mine.

1723.

Women's bodies are controlled for a reason.

And that reason isn't morals or religion or even protection-
those are *cover-ups*.
The reason women's bodies are controlled
is patriarchy.

The system is sexist- that is all.

And they use whatever means they can
(from marketing to religion to laws to morals to science to nature)
to try to gaslight us into believing there is a logic to the system.

But it's not logic, it's patriarchy.

And just like we learned it, we can unlearn it.

***

Repeat each word *consciously*:
I am **not** the misogyny
enforced on me.
I am free.

1724.

Non-men
can internalize patriarchy.

Non-Whites
can internalize White supremacy.

Non-heterosexuals
can internalize heteronormativity.

The oppressor
encourages the oppressed
to internalize
to normalize
to no longer realize
oppression.

***

Signs you've internalized misogyny:
-You base your value on your physical appearance (and judge other women that way).
-You give, but feel guilty to take.
-You feel shame about sex, but struggle to say no when your partner wants it.
-You think marriage and motherhood are your ultimate destination.

1725.

Maybe the wolf didn't eat the grandmother.

Maybe the grandmother ate the wolf,
and she's enacting on her granddaughter
everything that he is.

There are women who eat the wolf;
those are the women who digest patriarchy
and internalize misogyny.

There are women who eat the wolf;
those are the women who carry the wolf to every woman's space
and that's how the wolf
stays safe.

***

My grandmother taught me about shame.
Like all the good women,
who kept good to their name.
The women entrusted to be
the soldiers of patriarchy
the ones men would point at to say
"look, women have done this to you- not me".

Shame isn't something innate to women
we pass on what we learn about ourselves from men;
I was taught to keep my legs together purposely
that my vagina holds secrets

and my sanitary pads are dirty.
I was taught that honour is not a thing but a place
located exactly between the valleys of my thighs.
I was taught no strangers or lovers are allowed to visit
or even a kindly passerby.
Only husbands who had the keys to our fathers' hearts
are the men whom for
our thighs would part.

No one cares about women's hearts
for they want our bodies
not what beats inside them-
they want to take our pleasure
and give us the pain of breeding men.

Shame is weaved
so perfectly into your skin-
if a **thread** begins to **bare** flesh
that **threadbare** is sin.

But as I got older I would no longer listen.

Oh, grandma, there is no such thing as shame-
it is just blame
that we're supposed to welcome in.

***

There is no divine nature to patriarchy.
Women are taught to accept it.

The sacrifices
of our grandmothers
will not be passed on
to our daughters.

1726.

I don't want women to rule the world.

For centuries, women have internalized patriarchy too.

What makes you think those women can make the world better for you?

The world won't change if we change the gender of who rules.

The world will change only if we change the rules of gender.

1727.

At some point, women fully learn to hate themselves.

This is achieved through a disconnection between body and brain.

At some point,
women learn to view their bodies as necessary
and their brains as accessory.
That our appearance must be sculpted into beauty standards,
but we must never ever *think*...that we're beautiful.

We're kept on our toes that way.

We're kept searching for love and hating ourselves.

At some point, women fully learn to hate themselves.

And when they fully internalize this misogyny-
that's when they also stop seeing misogyny.

That's when misogyny kills us,
and we die every day trying to figure out what kills us.

1728.

They thought we'll become
just like our mothers;
silent and resilient.

But here we are
just like our fathers;
shaming our feminine
and embracing our masculine.

***

We measure a woman's liberation
by whether she works outside the house,
whether she gave up on makeup,
whether she prefers flats over high heels.
We use, what is traditionally deemed masculine,
as our standard yardstick to measure women's liberation.

Here's a radical idea:

Perhaps women's liberation
isn't about *adopting* the masculine,
but about questioning why liberation
requires *abandoning* the feminine?

1729.

Oh what a world-
it puts women in high heels
and skirts that twirl,
and then mocks them
for *running like a girl*!

***

Patriarchy hates femininity.
But also expects women
to embrace femininity to be desirable.

How fucked up is that?

Misogyny isn't only about hating women,
but about teaching them that they'll be loved
when they embrace this hate.

N.B. Let's heal our feminine from the hate of patriarchy.

1730.

Misogyny isn't only about hating women,
but about teaching them to hate themselves.

To view their gender as a less than.
To view the feminine as inferior:
Pink is "girly" (in a bad way),
makeup is vanity,
and fashion is silly.

We are taught that smashing those stereotypes
means we have to be "not like other girls"-
and yet ironically we must still be feminine
to win at the "pick me" game.

Misogyny isn't only about hating women,
but about teaching them to hate themselves in such a way
that they learn to accept the way the world hates women.

***

When we teach girls that they can wear blue,
while we don't teach boys that they can wear pink too;
we aren't empowering the feminine-
we're erasing it.

***

If you think skirts are for women but pants are for everyone
OR if you think high heels are for women but flats are for everyone
then you need to re-consider the difference between
gender neutrality vs. assimilation into patriarchy.

N.B. M&M announced that its female chocolate characters will no longer wear high heels in an effort to appear gender-neutral. But why can't high heels be seen as gender-neutral?

1731.

Who says feminists don't like to wear pink, or lipstick, or fashion?

It is misogynists who lumped those things as "feminine"
and equated "feminine" with "women"
and "women" with "weak",
and said feminists are fighting this "weak".

Feminists aren't at war with pink, or lipstick, or fashion-
they're at war with the misogyny that lumps those things
as "feminine"
and equates "feminine" with "women"
and "women" with "weak".

***

Female= sex assigned at birth
Girl/ woman= gender identity
Femininity= gender expression

Patriarchy has convinced us
that those categories are a *sequence*
(female=girl/ woman=femininity)
but they are *separate* categories.
The sequence is purely
a patriarchal social construction.

N.B. The Guevedoces are a community in the Dominican Republic
where individuals assigned female at birth develop a penis at puberty.

1732.
There are cisgender women who deny the oppression of transgender women on the basis that oppression is linked to our *assigned sex*- that women are oppressed because they are assigned *female* i.e. because of our biology, because we get periods and get pregnant.

But what about our *gender*?

Cis women are oppressed as a gender too. Because regardless of whether they get their period or get pregnant, they are still oppressed e.g. cis women who never got their periods, or cis women who struggle with fertility, or menopausal cis women- all are still oppressed. In fact, the discrimination they experience might even be greater than women who menstruate and get pregnant because they're looked down upon for not fulfilling/ no longer useful in their roles as child bearers in patriarchy.

And so the same can be said of transgender women. Their oppression is linked to their gender.

***

There are cis women
who take offense with terms like
"menstruating *people*/ pregnant *people*" etc.
As if cis women who menstruate or get pregnant
aren't fundamentally…
people?!

Inclusive language is important to acknowledge
that not everyone who gets their period or gets pregnant
identifies as a cis woman.
Also not all who identify as cis women
get periods or get pregnant,
and that doesn't make them any less of a woman.

What is so offensive about being inclusive of people
who don't fit the gender binary or patriarchy's biology?

Aren't we all fighting this harmful belief system?

N.B. There is no scientific case to exclude trans girls from girls'
sports teams. See: https://www.scientificamerican.com/article/trans-
girls-belong-on-girls-sports-teams/

1733.

Women don't have to...
*be defined by their bodies
*be cisgender
*have sex for reproduction
*sign up for marriage or motherhood
*cook or clean or smile
*endure abuse as a determinant of strength
*fulfil misogynistic expectations

It's 2022. Get onboard.

1734.

The women, who try to fit in patriarchy, will disappear within it.

You're not like other girls?
Other girls will continue to be like you.

You want to be a 'pick me'?
You will lose yourself to win a man who would never pick you over himself.

The women, who try to fit in patriarchy, will disappear within it.

And the irony is that they try to fit in patriarchy,
because disappearing is their worst fear.

***

The patriarchy loves it so much
when women internalize misogyny.
So that we begin fighting one another
instead of fighting patriarchy!

N.B. That is why "catfights" are romanticized (even sexualized) in the media, movies, and in our lives.

1735.

"You're not like other girls" is not a compliment.

It's a divide-and-conquer strategy.
It's how you internalize misogyny and settle into patriarchy.
It's how you subtly but surely end up disregarding the power of
sisterhood
by fighting one another over who is better,
instead of fight for each other together.
It's how you don't see that every freedom you have today was once
fought for by "other girls" who just "like you"- want to live better.

You are like other girls.
We must stick together.

                              ***

I am like other girls;
because when we're all taught
that we're 'unlike' one another,
what bonds us *horrifically* becomes
that we all 'dislike' one another.

And this is how we internalize misogyny.
This is how *all girls* inevitably suffer.

1736.

They make you believe
that women in the West
are the least oppressed,
but this is a misconception at best.
Because even though
they may struggle less
than the rest,
they're still oppressed-
and looking up to them
makes us lower the standards
for the freedom all women can expect.

***

How can some oppressions be seen as "better" than others
when all oppression is connected to the same root?

The misogyny in our world
that calls women "bitches" and silences them,
is the same one that once called women "witches" and executed them.

1737.

All women
internalize misogyny;
it is fed to us daily.

Spit it out.
Speak out.

If you have to- shout.

No more poisoned minds.

                    ***

Gentle reminder:

Women with internalized misogyny
aren't the enemy of feminism-
they are victims of patriarchy.
The enemy of feminism is patriarchy.

The woman who internalized misogyny is not your enemy.
The woman who upholds patriarchy is not your enemy.
She, too, is a victim of patriarchal conditioning erroneously thinking
her silence is a small price to pay for survival.
Directing your anger at her
distracts you from directing your anger at patriarchy.

And, inadvertently, you end up circulating the cycle of misogyny.

Women are **victims** of this patriarchal system,
it's important we don't hold them accountable
for internalizing misogyny
because it keeps us busy reproducing further misogyny
instead of looking at the core of the problem
and smashing patriarchy.

***

Women's internalized misogyny
is also a men's issue;
it is patriarchy that invents, normalizes, and teaches women to accept
misogyny.

Blaming women for internalized misogyny is victim blaming- it
derails accountability away from men who invented and uphold
misogyny.

1738.

Are women responsible too for the *continuation* of patriarchy?

No. I used to think that they are. But now I realize we need to be aware of how this system works in order not to victim blame.

The patriarchy is built by men- and yes, **it is upheld by *both* men and women**.

However men uphold because they benefit, women uphold because they are trying to *survive*. It is important to recognize those differences. And also it is important not to wish-wash the origins here- the patriarchy is not a system built by or for women.

Women are victims of patriarchy and when they uphold it they are trying to survive within it- because they will be punished otherwise. Women are rewarded by patriarchy for upholding it (through love, acceptance, proximity to power, money, etc.) which conditions them to continue to uphold as opposed to face the punishments for dismantling (which includes shaming, ostracizing, criminalizing, and killing of women).

It is derailing and dangerous to place equal responsibility on women and men for the continuation of patriarchy; because if men didn't invent it, women wouldn't internalize it. And if men didn't impose it, women wouldn't uphold it.

The point I want to make is this: There would be NO REASON for women to uphold patriarchy if men weren't enforcing it.

***

When women internalize patriarchy,
they do it to survive.
When men internalize patriarchy,
they do it to thrive.

And the tragedy
is that under patriarchy
none of us come out alive.

1739.

The patriarchy hurts men
by not allowing them
to wear pink or cry,
but it hurts women
by allowing men
to enslave women until they die.

We're both fighting the same patriarchy
but it's not the same fight.
Men are fighting to free themselves
women are fighting to be free from men.

Men kill themselves for patriarchy,
women are killed by it.

There is a difference.

1740.

Women don't *support* patriarchy.
They try to *survive* within patriarchy.

There's a difference.

Women internalize patriarchy with compliance
because they get punished for defiance.

Women internalize patriarchy to survive,
while men internalize it to thrive.
When women don't internalize patriarchy,
acceptance is taken away.
When men don't internalize it,
power is taken away.

But what is acceptance
when it is conditional upon denying yourself?
And what is power
when it is conditional upon conformity?

We all pay something to uphold patriarchy-
but the question is who can afford it?

Women fight to live.
Men live to fight.

For freedom,
women must be liberated from men
while men must be liberated from themselves.

1741.

So many women uphold patriarchy
because they are conditioned to believe
that the rewards they gain for compliance
are *privileges*.

***

"Beauty privilege" is what patriarchy calls it when it takes advantage
of women and expects them to be grateful for it.

Beauty privilege isn't a thing.

Women do not have privilege in the patriarchy.
They are, at best, merely rewarded for compliance
to condition them to accept the system.

***

It baffles me when people use the term "beauty privilege" to refer to
how the patriarchy favours women who conform to beauty standards.

Is it beauty *privilege* or beauty *currency*?

Privilege implies you have an advantage without being taken
advantage of.

But beautiful women don't have that.

What they have is terms of exchange.
Give their beauty, and get X Y Z.

***

While the "blonde" is the archetype of beauty standards,
the "dumb blonde" is an essential stereotype to go alongside.

Because if women are beautiful, they must be stupid. Right?

Do you see what women pay for their beauty *privilege*?

1742.

"Women don't have to go to war- that's privilege"
Do you know what happens to women during war though? Rape.
The same soldiers that throw bombs at your homes are exploding
inside women's bodies.

"Women get free entry to night clubs- that's privilege"
Do you know what women *bring* that the club views as value
enough to forgo the money? Themselves. The more women in the
club, the more likely men would want to pay for entry. We are not
getting in for free- we're used as a marketing scheme for free.

"Women aren't expected to be the breadwinner- that's privilege"
Do you know how that expectation, for centuries, has kept us
dependent on men (even toxic men) for survival and made it
impossible for us to leave and survive on our own? We still carry that
generational trauma. We still aren't paid equally to men. And so many
of us who want to be breadwinners are still deprived from that choice.

Women don't have any privileges in the patriarchy. That word,
privilege, is used to distract us from realizing the worst hidden costs.

***

"Marriage benefits women by giving them protection" they say.

So I tell them: But don't forget that the patriarchy that invented marriage, also invented the structures that women require protection from in the first place.

"Capitalism benefits women by giving them financial independence" they say.

So I tell them: But don't forget that it also ensures we stay dependent by paying us less for the work we do in the office and not paying us at all for the labour we do home.

N.B. We need to fiercely question patriarchal and capitalist structures that claim to benefit women. Nothing benefits women under patriarchy and capitalism.

1743.

"Men have it hard, too", he says, to refute feminism.
"Men go to war and die.
Men aren't allowed to cry.
Men lose cases of child custody".

So I tell him:
"I am glad you can see-
that the male privileges you enjoy in every other sphere
aren't free.
There is a price you have to pay
to uphold your patriarchy".

Women never asked men to go to war and die.
Women never asked men to not be emotional or not to cry.
Women never asked men to be sole breadwinners, while women
dominate child custody.
Women never asked for any of this shit that men complain about-
which is caused by their patriarchy.

***

Who says men are the stronger sex?
Patriarchy.

Who expects the stronger sex to be violent?
Patriarchy.

Who mocks the stronger sex for being violated?
Patriarchy.

Who, thus, makes it hard for violated men to speak out?
Patriarchy.

Who's saying patriarchy hurts all of us?
Feminism.

***

Q: So does feminism liberate men?
A: It's an inevitable outcome.

When we fight toxic masculinity to liberate women from its harms,
men are liberated from its expectations too.

1744.

"Queens were more likely to engage in war than kings", is a statement ripped out of context from a historic study that found that:

1) Unmarried queens were more likely to be attacked than kings because of the gender stereotypes that women (and especially single women) are "weak"- thus prompting queens to fight and fight back.

2) Married queens were more likely than married kings to put their spouses into positions of power to help them rule. Those discriminatory gender norms resulted in division of labour under queen reigns- which also enabled more participation in war than under king reigns.

N.B. See the historic study for further reading: Oeindrila Dube & S. P. Harish (2020), "Queens", Journal of Political Economy, University of Chicago Press, vol. 128 (7), pp. 2579-2652. DOI: 10.3386/w23337

1745.

The military draft of women isn't equality;
it is assimilation of women into patriarchy.

Fuck the patriarchy.

***

Male violence isn't normal; it's normalized.
Male violence isn't justifiable; it's justified.
There is a difference; it's our silence that creates indifference.

***

War is when the men in power
expect the men they empowered
to pay for that power with their lives.

Patriarchy hurts everybody.

N.B. Stand with the people of Ukraine.

1746.

Patriotism builds a sense of loyalty with one's land
and thus simultaneously a disloyalty of others.

Patriotism creates war.

Why are young men willing to die for a country
that is willing to send them to death?

No country that is willing to kill you for a piece of land
no country that values sand
over your soul,
is worth dying for.

***

At times of war, we can see how patriarchy hurts men too.

We can see how the men who call for war are never the ones to fight
in it.

We can see how the power of men is used to pay for the privilege of
the men in power.

We can see how power and privilege intersect to pick out whose
men's lives matter.

If war is noble…
why aren't the men calling for it also fighting on the frontlines?
Why are they sending other men to kill and die and call it
"patriotism"?

War is not patriotism; war is patriarchy.
And patriarchy isn't patriotic to anything other than power.

At some point you have to stop and realize how the men in power
abuse the power of men.

At some point you have to stop and realize how the power of men is
used to pay for the privileges of the men in power.

At some point you have to stop and realize that the patriarchy is
willing to kill everyone- even men- if that's the price to uphold
power.

1747.

Boys are told stories about saving the world
and girls are told stories about being saved by men,
and then
we grow up with this baggage;
men dream of war
while women dream of marriage.

Men have been lost in war
and women have been lost in marriage.
And the only difference is that men created war,
and women didn't create marriage.

***

Marriage is an institution of patriarchy that insists and persists on:

*The glorification of virginity for women (symbolized by the bride's white dress in the wedding)
*The simmering reality and legality of marital rape
*The girls sold as child brides and women forced in arranged marriages like a business deal
*The bride price/ dowry as a seal of payment for said business deal
*The women whose titles go from Miss to Mrs, give up their maiden names, and are named after their husband's like branded property of said business deal
*The expectation of women to perform unpaid labour in the marriage household

*The studies that show men are happier in marriage while women are miserable

***

"A woman's place is in the house"
is actually a pretty deadly statement
when you realize that the majority of women
are murdered in their homes.

N.B. A United Nations study found that the home is the most dangerous place for women because the majority of female homicide victims are killed by male partners and family members. (Source: https://www.unodc.org/unodc/en/frontpage/2018/November/home-the-most-dangerous-place-for-women-with-majority-of-female-homicide-victims-worldwide-killed-by-partners-or-family--unodc-study-says.html).

1748.

A society that celebrates women who get married and have kids,
but equally shames women who don't want those things-
isn't a society celebrating women.
It is conditioning them.

***

Marriage is not a choice for women in patriarchy.

Shaming women for being single, ensures they *get* married.
Shaming women for getting divorced, ensures they *stay* married.
Shaming women gives them no choice-
it conditions them what to choose.

***

To be wives and mothers is not the *destiny* of women;
it is the *destination* of patriarchy.

From a young age we're fed fairytales where romance and happy
endings culminate with us settling into roles prescribed by patriarchy.

As we get older, if we defy this script - we're shamed, blamed, even
criminalized. Whether we're called spinsters, selfish, forced into
marriage, or banned from abortion- there are people and laws pushing
us back down that very narrow aisle.

Women have died without knowing who wrote their ending.

"A woman's place is in the house"-
only when patriarchy's place is in the world.

"Marriage and motherhood are a woman's fate"-
only when patriarchy makes otherwise fatal.

***

Marriage and motherhood aren't the fate of women.

Abortion frees women from the destiny of motherhood.
Divorce frees women from the destiny of marriage.

A woman's destiny isn't tied to her womb or her heart-
it is tied by patriarchy.

Marriage and motherhood are a woman's destiny,
only if patriarchy is the destination.

1749.

If you celebrate women's choices
then you'll celebrate the woman
who picked herself over marriage
instead of calling her a spinster,
you'll celebrate the woman
who picked self-love
over an abusive partner
instead of shaming her for divorce,
you'll celebrate the woman
who picked her career
over starting a family
instead of asking her when (not *if*) she'll ever have a baby.

If you celebrate women's choices
you'll celebrate them for removing hijab
as much as for wearing it,
for belly dancing
as much as ballet.

If you celebrate women's choices
you won't choose for them
what or when or how or whether they're celebrated.

***

Women are slammed for choosing
a career over a family.

Women are slammed for choosing

a family over a career.

Women are slammed for choosing
to balance a career and a family.

No matter what we choose
we're slammed for *choosing*.

Read that again.

We're slammed because we're *choosing*.

Women aren't supposed
to have or make choices in patriarchy.

1750.

If you don't celebrate women being promoted
the way you celebrate them being proposed to,
and if you don't celebrate women getting abortion
the way you celebrate them getting pregnant-
then you didn't ever celebrate *women*.
You celebrated what *men* do to women.

***

Marriage and motherhood
are the most celebrated events
in women's lives
for a reason.

Do you think the patriarchy will ever celebrate women
for roles that don't serve men?

Marriage benefits men not women.

Marriage gives men access to
domestic labour without them paying for it (unpaid labour of wives
and mothers),
sex without a proper application of consent (shady laws against
marital rape),
children they never carry but who carry their names.

And yet marriage is portrayed
as a woman's fairytale and happily ever after
while for men it's a trap?!

He is her *prince charming*.
She is his *ball and chain*.

Conditioning women to believe marriage
is their happy ending
is one of the biggest enslavements of patriarchy.

***

We must stop telling women
that marriage is their "happily ever after",
when our idea of marriage requires the sacrifices of women.

This "happily ever after"
belongs to men, to patriarchy, to capitalism-
to everyone but the women it's targeted at.

The phrase
"happily ever after"
romanticizes
the sacrifices
of women.

1751.

Fairytales tell us that women must be protected *by* men.
Real life shows us that women must be protected *from* men.
Fairytales tell us that women must be saved *by* marriage.
Real life shows us that women must be saved *from* marriage.

Fairytales warp our reality out of fear:
not the fear that men won't stand up *for* women,
but the fear that women will stand up *against* men.

***

Women don't choose marriage,
marriage chooses us.

Ever since childhood we're fed fairytales
about a woman living in disaster
and then the prince comes
and marriage becomes
her happily ever after.
But the reality of those tales is still pending
for they never show us what happens
after the happy ending.
From whose perspective
is marriage a happy ending?
Studies show that men are happier in marriage
but women are miserable.
Our definition of *happily ever after*
is deeply patriarchal.

We don't choose marriage,
marriage chooses us.

We have to wait for a man to go down on one knee and propose,
our status is "miss"- as if there's something we "*miss*ed"-
until a man changes this
by declaring we're the one he chose.
We have to wait for men to choose
men who can't recognize us
outside of glass slipper shoes.
Men who just want a vagina to fuck
and children to claim and wives to abuse.

We don't choose marriage,
marriage chooses us.

We don't choose to do the housework that doesn't get paid,
we don't choose to spread our legs when our husbands want to get
laid,
we don't choose, we just do.
We're taught that's what we should do.

We don't choose marriage,
marriage chooses us.

And the biggest conspiracy
is when we
believe this whole narrative
was written romantically
for us.

***

If my kiss
has the power
to turn a frog into a prince;
then I'm the saviour
I'm the hero
then I didn't need him
for a happily ever after
he's the one who needed me.

What do I get for kissing the frog?
A prince who thinks my happily ever after is achieved through
serving him with my body and life for the rest of my life?

Fuck your fairytales.

1752.

When my husband visits my family
they roll out the red carpet.

They serve him tea
the way he likes it to the T.
They let him be,
they let him talk
about his leisure, about his work
and listen without judging.
I used to think it's just because
my family are so super loving.

When I visit my husband's family
all I'm served is shame.
Why did you do this? Why don't you do it like this?
Why did you do this again?
Lots of strategies of subtle and obvious blame.
I couldn't be myself ever
I was never good enough for his mother.
I used to think it's just because
his family hate me.

But you see.

After a while
I began to notice that this is a pattern
that happens
in almost every house in town;
a husband is welcomed by his wife's family,
but she is treated by his family with a frown.

Why?

My mother says it's because a woman's family don't want their
daughter to get divorced
so they treat her husband like a God
in hopes that he'll pass this treatment to their daughter.
But his family
don't care if his wife is happy,
because if she wants to leave
he can divorce her without stigmatizing himself,
and he'll easily re-marry.

This is patriarchy.
This is how our lives
are run and ruined by misogyny.

***

If marriage was *for women*
they wouldn't be made to take *vows*
of obedience.

1753.

If marriage is an institution
based on love and romance
as we're led to believe,
then gay couples
wouldn't have to fight so hard for the right to get married.

But marriage is an institution
based on preserving gender roles
and heteronormative patriarchy.

That is why gay couples weren't
(and in so many countries still aren't)
allowed to get married.

***

The fairytale wedding and the honeymoon
are periods of assimilating women
into the roles patriarchy has scripted for them.

For a few months of party and holiday
women are bribed into selling
the rest of their lives
to a system
that will work them (as free labour)
to death and until they die.

N.B. Is it "till death *do us* part" or "till death *does its* part"?

1754.

Marriage is a patriarchal and capitalist invention.

Marriage was invented by patriarchy to ensure men have ownership of women's sexual activity and ultimately reproductive rights. Because when you control reproduction, you can control not only women but also the repopulation, and thus control capitalism.

That's basically it.

When you understand that, you will see why virginity culture puts emphasis on "saving yourself until marriage" to "gift your virginity to the deserving man", while totally disregarding what a woman may want to do sexually.

You will see why marriage is presented in every culture as the end goal for women, while totally disregarding what a woman may want to do with her life. Divorce is shamed and spinsterhood is shamed to push women to marriage.

You will also see why having children outside of marriage makes those children "illegitimate" (because they only belong to their mother- and women shouldn't own the lineage) and why abortions are shamed and often criminalized- pushing women to have children, while totally disregarding whether a woman actually wants to have children.

Only when we see marriage as an option and not an expectation for women, we begin to untangle so much of this conditioning.

Women have the right to not want marriage or children.
Women have the right to want sex without marriage.
Women have the right to not want their fate to be tied to the fathers of their children

***

Male lineage is a patriarchal and capitalist invention.

Female lineage makes so much more sense because you can identify who the child belongs to based on the body that carried it. Women never need to "prove" whether a child is theirs because the evidence is carried by our bodies; only men require that proof. Thus patriarchy placed value on identifying the father of the child rather than the mother and invented male lineage. If the father cannot be identified then the child is deemed illegitimate, and if the mother doesn't marry the father then the child is deemed illegitimate too – the "bastard child" is a patriarchal invention to push women into marriage.

Male lineage is an invention that is patriarchal and capitalist- it stems from a time when only men were allowed to own property, and male lineage is the way for men to ensure that only their blood (male) heir inherited that property.

1755.

I am a woman
which means
my orgasms don't lead to procreation
they are purely for my pleasure-
and yet men shame me for wanting that pleasure.
They even went as far as banning me from abortion
when I want sex without wanting to be a mother!

I am a woman
which means
my body is the evidence
to show whether a child is mine-
and yet men call that child "illegitimate"
without evidence of male lineage.
They even went as far as developing paternity tests!

What a mess!

Men cannot have what I have
and they want I have-
so they call me weak, convince me to believe it, and oppress me
and then take all I have
away from me.

And then on top of that
Freud tells them
I've got "penis envy".

What a fucking frenzy!

1756.

I don't like the idea of marriage.

I don't like the idea of a law
governing my romantic relationship-
I want to feel free to enter/ exit a romantic relationship
with nothing binding me
the way I do for friendships
and other non-romantic relationships.

The institution of marriage forces you
to stay with one person for a legally binding happily ever after-
but I like the idea that my partner is with me
out of their own will
and not because it is legally binding.

I like the idea that if we were ever unhappy together
we can walk away,
without waiting for a court to grant us permission.

I hate the idea of a law telling me
who I can and cannot fuck,
and when and whether I can leave.

***

I never wanted marriage.

I wanted sex.

But I was taught that
I cannot
should not
must not
have sex outside marriage.

I was taught that sex outside marriage is the biggest sin.
That I'd breach my family's honour with a broken hymen.

There was so much trauma that they labelled under my name.
There was so much guilt and shame;
they packed it and I carried.

And so when I wanted to have sex,
I got married.

***

Honour killings
are based on the premise that
a woman having premarital sex
is something that is more dishonourable
than the murder of said woman.

1757.

Women should not be valued based on virginity
not just because
virginity is a social construct,
but also because
value is a social construct.

***

She didn't realize
that she was circumcised.

It was done when she was
too young to know,
and as she got older
silence was all she saw.

She didn't know they used a *saw*.

No one talks about
what female anatomy should look like
only that good women must not lust or like
sex.
That's all her sex education.
She didn't know about infibulation.
She thought her mutilated vulva
was just God's creation.

How could she know?

She never even had a chance to say NO.

1758.

The first lesson women learn about sex is that we have no choice.

We're taught to "save our virginity",
instead of asked whether we want to or not.

We're taught sex is "penis in vagina",
instead of asked what kind of sex we want.

We're taught sex is something we give,
instead of asked what we want to take out of it.

We learn that we have no choice,
when we're never asked for consent.

We're taught that having a say and having desires,
makes us sluts.

We learn that our consent
is something worse than our choices being taken away.

There is a voice- their voice- in our minds constantly screaming
"if you want sex, you're a slut".
How can we consent? When we're taught not to.
How can we enjoy? When we're shamed for it.

We learn it's scary to say "no",
just like it's shameful to say "yes".

***

The same ideology that says women
shouldn't have sex before marriage,
also (not so coincidently)
wouldn't address lack of female pleasure within marriage.

They have an issue not with sex,
but with women's pleasure from sex.

If a boyfriend touches her body- she's committed a sin.
If he becomes her husband- she's made into an "honest woman".
What's the difference between those two relationships
besides a man being granted her legal ownership?

We teach a girl that if she consents to sex outside marriage,
she's *damaged goods*.

If she touches herself with pleasure,
she's *damaged goods*.

Even if she gets raped,
she's *damaged goods*.

The only time she isn't *damaged goods*
is when she's taken by a husband.

Even if he doesn't pleasure her,
even if he rapes her,
even if he *damages* her *for good*…

He's still her husband, so it's all *good*.

***

The brain is the biggest sex organ.

When one is taught to think that sex is bad for all their life, they won't suddenly be able to feel good about sex once they are married. This mutilation of sexual pleasure continues within marriage.

Abstinence ideology trains women not to want sex. And perhaps that's the goal in a patriarchy. For women not to *have* sex, but to *give* sex. For women not to think about sex at all; but to be incubators for male pleasure and sperm.

N.B. A woman is four times more likely to be raped by her husband or ex-husband than by a stranger. Furthermore, 77% of marital rape goes unreported to police. (Source: https://www.refinery29.com/en-us/marital-rape-in-relationships-statistics).

1759.

If you shame women for consenting to sex,
you're saying that women's consent to sex is shameful.

And if you're saying that women's consent to sex is shameful,
then you're also saying you'd rather rape women.

***

When you teach girls
to guard their virginity until marriage,
you also teach them
to **withhold consent** before marriage
and **have no consent** within it.

You are conditioning their consent.

Being taught to say no *until* you're in a marriage,
also means do not say no in a marriage.

And that is why the concept of consent is absent in so many
marriages.

***

Women are taught
that they *lose value*
when they *lose virginity*,
but not if that virginity is lost
within a heterosexual marriage.
Which is to say that virginity
isn't about women *losing value*,
but about men *gaining control*.

N.B. See #MarriageStrike on Twitter where Indian men are threatening to go on a "marriage strike" because the courts were looking to criminalize marital rape in India.

1760.

"I took her v-card" he proudly boasts.

So I tell him:
Oh you *took* her "v-card"?
Did you try using it?
Did it work anywhere?
Did you try using it at the ATM?
Did it get you any money?
Did you try using it at the library?
Did it get you any books?
Maybe try using it for the gym?
What?
It didn't get you in?!
Damn!
Show me the card! Where is it? Come on...Hold it out for me.
Oh you can't?
Why?
Because it doesn't actually exist and is merely a product of your imagination?

You didn't take anything from her.

***

"Losing your virginity"
isn't actually a thing.

Your virginity isn't in a "lost & found" repository.

To "lose your virginity", you need to have found it first
and chances are you didn't even consider "finding your virginity"
until the heteronormative patriarchy told you to look for it.

And where is it? No one knows for a fact.

No medical test, penis, or blood-stain can "find" your virginity
because your virginity isn't "lost"; it isn't real.

You *lose* nothing the first time (or any time) you have sex;
you *gain* sexual experience.

The only way to truly
"lose your virginity"
is to literally
"lose your [*ideas of*] virginity".

***

Virginity culture
teaches women to think of consequences
"so what will happen, if I have sex?"
while it teaches men to think of experiences
"so what, if I happen to have sex?"

***

242

"Marrying a non-virgin is like buying a used car-
who wouldn't want a new car?" he asks so sly.

So I reply:
"Fuckboy this isn't about you
I'd rather test drive- try that gear stick
before I buy."

***

My sexual experience is not like chewing gum!
Goddammit!

It is not a lock that can be opened by any key
it is not a piece of paper when scrunched it cannot be
it is not a precious jewel to reward a man for what he can be
it is not a car, when used, it loses retail value.

My sexual experience is not a metaphor
for the way you want to objectify me.

And just like
your penis doesn't get *narrow* from fucking,
my vagina doesn't get *loose* from fucking.
Sex doesn't change our genitals;
misogyny changes our perceptions.

No changes happen in a woman's *vagina*
the first time (or any time) she has sex;
the changes happen in the *minds*
of misogynists.

No changes happen in a woman's *body*
if she wears a revealing dress;
the changes happen in the *minds*
of misogynists.

1761.

He calls my body a "sin"
as *he* gazes at it with *his* growing erection.

"So YOU'RE going to hell!"- I tell him.

***

You love to fuck her
and when you do
you hate her and call her impure.

That's cognitive dissonance for sure.

If her value decreases
because she had sex with you
then you're literally saying
YOU decreased her value.

Check yourself.

***

Virginity is a concept created by men
who think their penises are so dirty
they make a woman impure.

Because "virginity"
cannot be
explicitly
used to control women
without the implicit belief that
penises are so dirty
since that's what allegedly
makes a woman
lose her purity.

***

Her vagina makes him a stud,
but his penis can only make her a slut.
Which is to say you cannot call her **"dirty"**
without also willing to imply that **"penis"** is dirty.

Because this is how patriarchy works:
it is willing to hurt men
if this helps sustain the oppression of women.

1762.

"Penis in vagina" sex
is necessary for procreation
but not necessary for pleasure.

Let's realize those are two different things.

***

Imagine if women aren't taught to "save their virginity",
but asked whether we want to or not?

Imagine if women aren't taught that sex is "penis in vagina",
but asked what kind of sex we want?

Imagine if women aren't taught that sex is something we *give* to
reward "good men",
but asked what we want to *take* out of it?

Imagine if women are taught that their consent and pleasure is
imperative in sex,
how many of us would recognize that everything we've normalized
about sex is actually...our conditioning from rape culture?

1763.

The desire for a "tight" vagina stems from rape culture.
A vagina that is aroused and ready for sex is not "tight".

***

The myth that "penetrative sex the first time is painful for women/ people with vaginas" is based on romanticising rough penetration without achieving a proper level of arousal for the vagina. And the pain that actually occurs is more to do with that rough entry while you weren't properly aroused as opposed to it being your first time. But you usually don't know that when it's your first time. So you believe the myth and blame it on it being your first time, as opposed to realizing you had a selfish partner.

***

We're erroneously taught that penetrative sex, for women and people with vulvas, is supposed to *hurt* the first time.

But sex isn't what hurts- it's the fact that the dick isn't waiting for you to be turned on enough before penetration.

Sex isn't what hurts- it's that you being tight is seen as a flex rather than a sign that more foreplay is needed.

Sex isn't what hurts- it's that porn has normalized viewing your pain as pleasure, your groans as moans.

Sex isn't what hurts- misogyny is.

***

First you "lose" your virginity,
then you're "loose",
then you "lost" your value.

How can women "gain" pleasure from sex
when we're wired to believe sex is a "loss" for us?

1764.

They want us to be virgins
but also know how to please a man in bed.
They want us to be inexperienced about our own pleasure,
so that we only experience theirs.

***

Imagine if, during sex,
men moaned when we didn't even touch their spots.

Imagine if men accepted every kink *just because*
we told them it's hot.

Imagine if men aren't expected to express sexual desire
of *anything* beyond what we do to them.

Imagine if, during sex,
men behaved the way porn depicts women.

1765.

I wish that every girl knows
sex isn't something done to you.
You're not supposed to be spread under a man
that you'll never get over
how he used you,
how you watched him pleasure himself
how you believed this was sex
you never said yes- *you were taught to say yes*
to this selfish performance of incompetence.

I wish that every girl knows
her body isn't a tool for male masturbation
that she has a human right to hesitation
because with all the false narratives
it's not always a clear declaration.
Boys and men notoriously dismiss the situation.

I wish that every girl knows
her pleasure is a revolution.
That she doesn't lose anything with her virginity
because she is like the ocean;
the same water cannot be touched twice.

I wish that every girl knows
that no girl is born a virgin
in a patriarchy that has fucked us with lies.

1766.

Let's teach our daughters
that boys are damaged goods after sex
that they are good for nothing else
that their purpose is to look fine
that they must cook and clean all the time.

Let's teach our daughters about boys
the same bullshit we teach our sons about girls-
and let's see how many generations it would take
to destroy this "man's world".

***

Imagine if we tell men their first ejaculation has virgin semen that
would be forever lost if they masturbate OR they need to save it for
the right woman as it's their most prized possession OR they're
damaged goods if they lose it outside marriage and no one would ever
want to marry them OR women can definitely tell if they lost it
because sex would feel different OR the more they ejaculate the
narrower their penises get OR subject them to virginity testing by
doctors who check if that virgin semen is intact.

Imagine if for thousands of years men are taught those myths- and we
all uphold them today under the guise of protection, religion,
morality, safety, and science.

If imagining that sounds absurd and cruel to men, why can't we realize that it is absurd and cruel that we're still doing this to women?

1767.

Please believe me.

I beg her.

Please believe me,
this body of yours carries no shame
there is no honour for men to claim
there is no family name
etched or sketched
between your thighs.

This is all patriarchy.
Patriarchy is married to misogynistic lies.

**

How did we turn women enjoying sex
into an insult (slut)?

How did we turn women speaking out
into a vice (bitch)?

How did we turn the organ that pushes humans out to life
into a weakness (pussy)?

How did we stop seeing things as they are
to believe lies invented by patriarchy?

N.B. In 2011, a Saudi cleric warned that allowing Saudi women to
drive cars would lead to the "end of virginity".

1768.

Virginity is the **product** of patriarchal **imagination**--
in which woman is conditioned to believe
that she is the **product**
and her desire is **imagination**.

***

Virginity was invented
to stop women from *having* sex.

Abortion bans are implemented
to stop women from *enjoying* sex.

Slut-shaming is enforced
to stop women from *consenting* to sex.

And when you don't believe that women should
have, enjoy, and *consent* to sex;
you also won't believe that a woman expressing her sexuality
in any way
is doing it, not for you, but for herself.

1769.

A woman's sexual desire is mutilated in the patriarchy,
so much so
that even when she acts upon it-
it is still assumed she is doing it for a man.

Never for herself.

It is hard to believe it is for herself,
when even "herself" is an asset owned by men.

***

Why can't you believe that she *reveals* her body to be empowered,
when you easily believe that man *revels* in her body to be powered?

***

We can't imagine a woman doing anything sexual
is doing it for herself
because we have normalized
that sex is something just for men.

While girls are saving themselves,
boys are masturbating to porn.

While girls are worrying about "losing" their virginity,
boys are excited to "score".

Women are slut-shamed for consenting to sex,
while men are seen as studs for it.

"Save sex for marriage" insinuates
that sex is the "worst" taboo for a woman to engage in,
but also the "best" gift she gives her husband.

**Women's sexuality is viewed as relational to men,
while men's sexuality is just a biological function.**

She is "asking for it" by wearing a sexy dress,
but he just has an erection he can't help it.

The damage this causes is far-reaching.

We must re-imagine women being sexual,
without it being about or for men.

We owe it to women.

***

Sex is not a reward
that women must give to good men

in return for love and respect.

Men get love and respect from us for free
and that's what we should expect
from them too.

1770.

Dear Cishet Men,

Has it occurred to you that women like sex too? Just like you, and in the same way that you do? That what makes you studs doesn't make us sluts- it makes us human too? That when we enjoy being sexy and being sexual, it's because we're doing it for ourselves not for you? That we also want to have sex just for pleasure not for kids? That our orgasms matter too? Has it occurred to you that sex isn't just something for you? To use women through?

Sincerely,

Women tired of explaining this shit to you.

P.S. How convenient is it
for you to pretend
that you don't understand consent
and can't find the clit?

P.S.S. Maybe the clit wouldn't be so hard to find if you stopped verbally mutilating it by referring to our vulvas as vaginas (the part useful to patriarchy for penetration and reproduction). Genitals aren't just for reproduction. No one says "ball sack" to refer to your penis.

1771.

Every time I orgasm
after masturbation,
my eyes roll so far back into my head
they become
one
with my mind.

Perhaps that's why they say
"masturbation makes you blind".

***

Women who feel "guilt/ shame" after masturbating
feel that way because *they have been taught*
that their pleasure should *induce* "guilt/ shame",
not because "masturbation" in itself
induces "guilt/ shame"...

1772.

"What turns you on?" he asked.
"Consent" I replied.

***

Women don't just want consent.
We also want orgasms.

Gaining our consent without giving us orgasms too,
means you're using our bodies
while perpetuating our pleasure as taboo.

***

My favourite position?
Being on top
of toppling
the patriarchy
that makes you ask me
such sexist questions.

1773.

If a girl is too young to have sex,
then surely she's too young
to be seen as sexual?
Yet so many young girls are sexualized.

If a girl is too young to be dating
then surely she's too young
to get married?
Yet so many young girls are child brides.

If a girl is too young to have a job,
then surely she's too young
to do the housework?
Yet so many young girls are performing domestic labour.

If a girl is too young, yet she's treated like a woman
then surely she's being groomed
to normalize oppression.

***

Patriarchy teaches us to "normalize" things
that aren't inherently normal.

Things like
victim blaming

body shaming
pleasure shaming
impossible ideals
housework being our duty
objectifying us
reducing us to our wombs
pushing us into marriage and motherhood,
etc. etc.

When we *question* those things-
we're treated as if we lost our minds
which leads to anxiety for us.

When we *defy* those things-
we're treated as outcasts
which leads to anxiety for us.

This not only impacts
our mental, emotional, and physical wellbeing-
but also creates generational trauma
that we pass on to other girls and women
and which ensures patriarchy continues living.

1774.

Marriage and motherhood
are roles;
patriarchy turned them
into goals.

1775.

If you're a mother
who doesn't feel "motherhood is a bliss"
I'm here to tell you this:
you're not crazy.

Motherhood is the most
tiring,
unappreciated,
and undervalued role that exists.

They tell you none of this...
so that you feel crazy
when you don't think it's "bliss".

N.B. If motherhood is bliss- why aren't men taught to aspire to it? If men want family so much why don't they play an active role in it? Or do they just want family as a way to keep women locked in the home?

1776.

Even when we feel ready and we *choose* motherhood, often times the reality of it is so much harder than you'd expect...and there should be no shame or guilt in saying we are exhausted or even have regrets- it doesn't mean we love our kids less, it means we are human capable of feeling the entire rush of emotions on this roller coaster.

***

Being a mother is a role that is valuable,
but it isn't what defines my value as a woman.

1777.

Mother and motherhood are two separate things.

I can want to be a mother out of my own desire, but with that I am thrust into motherhood. And motherhood is a patriarchal construct.

The roles of motherhood that I am expected to play as a mother (e.g. the unpaid labour, emotional labour, primary child-carer, etc.) is something patriarchal. And being reduced to motherhood as the only value we provide in society is also patriarchal.

***

There is something that isn't spoken about enough. So I'm going to say it clearly:

I love my kid, I hate motherhood.

How we mother- the physical, mental, and emotional labour isn't natural- it is something taught, conditioned, and ingrained into us by patriarchy. No one is born knowing how to cook, clean, run a household, and cater to infants with everything that it entails. It is taught. And only taught to girls and women. And thus we carry the burden of doing it all, and teaching it to our sons and husbands if we want to break the cycles.

N.B. Maternal instincts are a myth. Further reading:
https://www.healthline.com/health/parenting/maternal-instinct

1778.

Genitals aren't used to cook or clean
in fact we'd be worried about hygiene
if they are.

So why the fuck
is cooking/ cleaning a *female* job?

1779.

A man who cannot cook
isn't ready for marriage.

He's ready
for his first Easy-Bake Oven.

***

The reason why men aren't expected
to know how to cook and clean
to be eligible for marriage (while women are)
is because marriage under patriarchy
isn't viewed as a partnership
but a venture that relies on exploiting
the unpaid labour of women.

***

Perhaps men are always angry
because they're hungry
and they don't know how to cook
and women no longer want to make them sandwiches.

Perhaps men need to learn how to cook.

N.B. *Hangry* men will not change the world!

1780.

Why are basic life skills (cooking, cleaning, etc)
branded as feminine activities?

Why does toxic masculinity prevent men
from learning and practicing said activities?

Is it unmanly to try to survive?

When the patriarchy frames the survival skills
of cooking and cleaning as feminine,
it also frames them as emasculating for men.
In doing so, it keeps men dependent on women for basic survival.
Yet it won't admit it keeps men "dependant" on women-
instead it encourages men
to use violence, force, and control
to ensure they are served by women.

***

Patriarchy teaches men
to rely on women
for basic survival skills like cooking and cleaning.
And then (to guarantee men get served)
it absurdly tells women
that they are the ones who can't survive without men!

She's taught to cook and clean without the help of a man,
and yet told she can't survive without a man.

He's taught to rely on women's labour to cook and clean for him, and yet told he's the independent one.

Make it make sense.

1781.

Feminism has fought
to ensure women don't need to marry men for survival.

But toxic masculinity still won't even allow men
to learn how to cook, clean,
perform domestic work, and childrearing-
ensuring that men will always need women.

That is the problem.

While feminism empowers women,
toxic masculinity infantilizes men.

Good luck fellow men.

Let The Games Begin!

1782.

Toxic masculinity is the infantilization of men.

It tells men it's okay to yell and throw tantrums when you're upset.

It tells men it's okay to rely on someone else to cook and clean for them.

It tells men it's okay to go to war if you don't get what you want.

Ironically, to "man up" is to stay a child
while you're inside the body of a man.

**

Repeat after me:

Basic life skills have no gender.
Everyone needs to learn
how to cook, clean,
and put the spider out in the backyard.

1783.

It's not impressive
when a man can cook, clean, and take care of his kids-
it's basic.

Patriarchy trains us to think that basic,
when done by men, is impressive.
But when done by women, it's duty.

So that the bar is set to end for men
at exactly the point where it begins for women.

***

Some things considered "bare minimum" when done by wives, but
"praiseworthy" when done by husbands:
*Taking care of your own kids
*Cooking, cleaning and any basic household chores
*Prioritizing family over career
*Giving orgasms
*Being faithful
*Taking care of your partner in sickness
*Not being abusive or violent

1784.

He takes care of his kids?
Super dad!

She takes care of her kids?
Simply mom.

***

If we can accept a world
where women work outside the house
without appraise,
why can't we accept a world
where men work inside the house
without praise?

1785.

Women have always worked.

They weren't always *paid*.

Our work is still
unpaid at the home
underpaid at the office.
But women have always worked.

The difference between a woman who is working at home
and a woman who is a CEO at a company
is not the value of their labour-
but that society decided
whose labour is valued.

And the benchmark for that decision is based upon men's labour.

***

"Why is there a stigma that housework isn't "real work" and why do
men refuse to do it preferring an office job?" I was asked.

So I answered:

Housework is real work. The stigma that it isn't "real work" comes
from it being unpaid work- which is why men think they're too good
for it. Men are taught that their work is too valuable- they won't offer
their labour for free in patriarchy.

And the work women do at home is unpaid not because it isn't valuable- but because the women performing it aren't valued. It's the same reason why the work women do at the office is underpaid.

Raising children isn't free.
Breast milk isn't free.
Cooking/ cleaning isn't free.
Women's labour isn't free-
it's just that 'woman' isn't *valued*
by patriarchy.

1786.

Most chefs at restaurants are men paid top salaries,
and most cooks at home are women paid no (or low) salaries.

Whichever way you look at it-
the only explanation for this is misogyny.

Because this bizarre gender disparity
cannot be justified except with the equally bizarre notion
that one is perhaps using their genitals to prepare the food.
And if that's the case,
why are women's genitals not valued as much as men's?
So again, the only explanation for this is misogyny.

***

Everything women do at home for free,
patriarchy and capitalism offers it in the market
with a (often high) price tag.

Childcare?
Laundry?
Cleaning?
Cooking?
Teaching?
Entertaining?
Even sex?

So it's not that patriarchy and capitalism

don't recognize the value of the work that women do-
it's that they don't value the women doing it.

1787.

Motherhood is valuable in patriarchy;
but mothers aren't.
Because the use of women is valuable in patriarchy;
but women aren't.

Sexualizing women is valuable in patriarchy;
but sexual women aren't.
Because the use of women is valuable in patriarchy;
but women aren't.

***

The mother and the stripper
are both looked down upon,
because why would the patriarchy
look up to women whose labour
is essential
and thus let them realize
how much power they hold?

If she can run a household,
she can run the world.
If she can bring a man to his knees,
she can bring the downfall of patriarchy.

***

Perhaps sex work is stigmatized
because patriarchy wants us to give sex for free.

The same way they devalue the jobs
of being a housekeeper or a nanny-
but encourage mother's to do those exact things for free.

1788.

If women's unpaid labour
wasn't framed as moral duty;
how many of us would ignore
the dust on the floor,
and order takeout
without feeling guilty?

***

Mothers are made to feel guilty for resting (part of 'mom guilt')
because we're compared, not to the standards of men,
but of machines.

We're expected to do the
housework,
office work,
child care,
elderly care,
emotional labour,
all while being fit, pretty, and in the mood for sex.

We work 24/7 like a machine
and any stop point for rest is riddled with guilt.

Fuck, even machines can't perform all that.

A sex toy won't wash your clothes,
and a washing machine won't have sex with you.

The standards set for women
are beyond any expectation we set for anything.

***

In a world that exploits
your labour;
procrastination
is activism.

1789.

The training starts from a young age-
young girls are already performing household chores;
cooking, cleaning, and serving everyone in the house.
So that when they're older
they can only see their free labour
as moral duty.

***

'Woman', under patriarchy
is not merely a gender identity
but also a free labour resource.

The question "are you a stay-at-home or working mother?" is
redundant. All mothers are working mothers- and all sisters,
daughters, and wives are also all working to serve brothers, fathers,
and husbands.

The question is; why is our labour branded as a moral duty?
And the answer is; so that we don't expect to get monetary pay.

Because when women gain financial independence, the patriarchy
crumbles.

Women don't need patriarchy, but patriarchy needs women.
Our unpaid and overexploited labour oppresses us,
but our oppression is what the patriarchy needs to survive.

1790.

Mothers buy and wrap presents,
and their unpaid labour creates the holiday magic.
And then a cis White man called Santa takes all the credit.

Ho, Ho, Ho, Hold up...

Isn't this the best example of patriarchy, capitalism, and White
supremacy?!

***

In fairytales, women's labour is attributed to "magic".

Forest animals help Cinderella do the house chores
and a fairy godmother dresses her up with a magic wand.

In real life this is all women's hard work- the forest animals are
symbolism of the millions of ways women's hands and feet are
stretched to get the housework done, and the magic wand is the needle
of a very talented seamstress who studied her craft for years.

Attributing women's labour to *magic* is an attempt to make us believe
that women's hard work isn't something *real*.

1791.

"If he works full-time and she stays at home,
then she needs to do all the house chores-
that's EQUALITY!" he says.

So if he works 9-5 for 5 days a week
with weekends off and paid breaks-
can she also do the housework
from 9-5 for 5 days a week
with weekends off and paid breaks?
Or is she expected to work 24/7 (for free) inside the house
just because he works a few hours outside the house
and thinks a woman's job is to serve him?

Let's not normalize entitlement under the guise of EQUALITY.

***

Patriarchy treats women
the way capitalism treats any natural resource;
we are used and abused.
We give them life, like trees,
and they won't stop chopping us down.

1792.

Patriarchy treats women as commodities;
to be fucked, to produce children,
to do domestic work, to look appealing.

That is why our pleasure is shamed and our pain is romanticized.
That is why abortion is criminalized.
That is why our work is unpaid at home and underpaid at the office.

Any movement, like feminism, that recognizes our humanity
is a big NO
because it forces patriarchy to realize we are not commodities.

***

Every injustice women experience is due to our objectification.

Consent doesn't matter?
Because we're seen as objects and objects don't give consent.

Silenced?
Because objects don't speak.

Not believed?
Because objects don't speak let alone say truth.

Workplace discrimination?
Because objects aren't meant to go to work but to be used to work.

Imposed dress codes?
Because objects don't decide what to wear.

Women are *feeling* tired of all this.

And the fact that we're *feeling* means we're not objects.

And this upsets
the patriarchy
because it reminds them
that we aren't commodities.

1793.

Womanhood is not an occupation.

It is not my duty, as a woman,
to look pretty or cook or clean or reproduce.

It is not my duty, as a woman,
to please men; to smile at all of them or spread my legs for one of
them.

It is not my duty, as a woman,
to offer unpaid labour and accept underpaid labour.

Womanhood is not an occupation;
it is not my duty, as a woman, to retire my liberation.

***

Love is not a duty
that women must give men.

Obedience is not a duty
that women must give men.

Housework is not a duty
that women must give men.

Patriarchy invents those duties
and gives them to women.

1794.

I don't need to be paid to feel valued
(this is a capitalist idea)
but I need to be paid for my labour.

Free labour isn't how we fight capitalism.
Free labour is not something good for women.
Free labour only serves the selfish capitalist system.
Free labour means the poor get poorer.
Free labour means the oppressed get further marginalized.

If free labour is good, why don't men offer their labour for free?
If free labour is good, why don't the rich offer their labour for free?

The rhetoric of free labour as something good is often pushed at the
most marginalized: women.

Ask yourself; who benefits from women's free labour?

The love and care we're promised as a return- do not pay the bills.

Love and care may build a home
but will never buy a house.

And when women aren't paid for their labour
their destiny becomes tied to the house
and to the men who own it.

***

Perhaps we have to
teach ourselves how to
leave those dishes in the sink
instead of leave our dreams to sink.

1795.

Sometimes
I think about the women
who never were
who could have been,
who had the talent to
who were so keen
to do so much more than
keep the kitchen clean.

Sometimes
I look for the women
who were never seen
in the eyes of their daughters
and granddaughters.
I look for those women in ancestry lines-
that never made it into the family trees
as if they never existed, once upon a time.

How many women
have lived and died
spending sweat and blood on this earth,
without ever finding out
what their dreams were worth?

N.B. It is very common practice in Arab countries that women are
excluded from family trees, where only male lineage and
contributions are valued and traced.

1796.

My mother told me
that when she was 12
and people asked her
"what do you want to be
when you grow up?"

She'd say:
"A man.
I want to be a man".

And it's not that she does not
relate to her assigned gender identity;
she wanted to be a man
because she wants what men have
she wants to be free.

1797.

"Men created everything in the world!" he barked.

So I told him:
Men created everything in the world
because they stopped women from creating anything in the world.
They enslaved us in the homes
branded our unpaid labour as moral duty
underpaid us in factories
stopped us from education
and from voting for the people who will allow us to have an
education.
That's the history of our situation.
They stopped us from shattering glass ceilings
and put us into glass slippers
to polish glass floors.
Men closed on us all the doors.
Men didn't *create* everything in the world;
they *controlled* and still *control*
everything in the world.

"Men created everything in the world!" he still barked.

So I told him:
"Women created men".

***

"All of this world is *built and raised*
by men!" he says.

"And all of those men were *birthed and raised*
by women!" I say,
"so what's your point?"

"But what else have women accomplished?" he sneers.
"This world was built by men!
Everything you enjoy,
everything you use,
was built by men, provided to you by men
who you claim abuse!"
he continues.

"Yes they abuse" I say.
"I wonder
how many of our foremothers
who aren't here with us today,
would tell you about the dreams they had
buried under white dresses,
because it was so bad
for women to remain Misses!
I wonder how many of our foremothers
would have invented new roads and medicines
and paths to healing
if they weren't taught that their only role
is to be appealing
and find prince charming,
isn't it alarming
to you
how many inventions were built by men
do you wonder

where were the women?
Isn't this evidence of abuse when
half of the population built this world
while the other half weren't even heard?
They say give a woman seed
she'll turn it into life.
But if you take from a woman her dreams,
she'll turn into nothing more than a wife".

1798.

It is violence to re-frame
men's oppression of women in the house
as "men providing"-
there would be no need for men to be "providers"
if women were provided equal opportunity outside the house.

It is violence to re-frame
men's restriction of women's clothing and behaviour
as "men protecting"-
there would be no need for men to be "protectors" of women
if they weren't protecting patriarchy.

It is violence to re-frame
men's violation of women's consent
as "men pursuing"-
there would be no need for men to be "pursuers" of women
if they weren't pursuing control.

The "provider, protector, pursuer" narrative of men
is based on the "depriving, depraving, disregarding" of women.

***

While men thrive,
women are trying to survive.

He can get a raise at work,
because a woman is raising his children at home.

He can get ahead,
because a woman was pushed behind.

He is seen as stronger,
because he defines strength- and he decides everything to do with
women's power is a weakness.

Instead of saying "this is a man's world",
ask him how many women did he steal it from?

1799.

James Brown sang
"this is a man's world
but it would be nothing
without a woman or a girl".

But he didn't specify
that it's a *cishet* man's world.

And he didn't say *why*
it would be nothing without a woman or girl.

He didn't say it's only a man's world
because men gain their privilege by oppressing women and girls.

If you listen closely to this popular song
it's actually about how men
exploited and marginalized women
to build this "man's world".

***

REWRITING THE LYRICS [edits in parentheses]:

This is a man's world, this is a man's world
And [he wouldn't let] nothing, nothing [belong to] a woman or a girl

You see, man [didn't let woman] make the cars to take us over the

road
Man [didn't let woman] make the train to carry the heavy load
Man [didn't let woman] make electric light to take us out of the dark
Man [didn't let woman] make the boat for the water, like Noah [didn't let woman] make the ark

This is a man's, man's, man's world
Oh but [there's one thing, one thing to be done by] a woman or a girl

Man [gives woman the labour of] our little bitty baby girls and our baby boys
Man makes [his ego] happy, 'cause man made them toys
And after man makes everything, everything he can
You know that man makes money, to [keep woman dependent on] man

This is a man's world
And [he wouldn't let] nothing, nothing, not one little thing, [belong to] a woman or a girl
He's lost in the wilderness
He's lost in bitterness, he's lost lost…

1800.

"This is a man's world", they'll say
socially,
economically,
politically,
scientifically,
every luxury
it is built by men-
ALL MEN.

But when you want to hold them accountable
for its deeply flawed structures;
for discrimination,
for sexism,
for racism,
for classism,
for ableism,
for wars-
they tell you
NOT ALL MEN.

To the one holding
this "woman's book"
in a "man's world":

Take up space.

Made in the USA
Columbia, SC
15 September 2024

41840928R00181